# DEFIANCE
## ANARCHIST STATEMENTS
## BEFORE JUDGE AND JURY

detritus books
Olympia, WA

FIRST DETRITUS BOOKS EDITION, 2019

Published in the USA by Detritus Books

Cover art by Dylan Garrett Smith || dylangarrettsmith.com
Book design by Ben Cody

DETRITUS BOOKS
OLYMPIA, WA
detritusbooks.com

Distributed by AK Press

Detritus Books ISBN: 978-1948501071

Printed in Canada
10 9 8 7 6 5 4 3 2 1

*to the defiant.*

Enrique Flores Magón

ACTIONS MAY SPEAK LOUDER THAN WORDS. BUT OCCASIONALLY, someone's words come in a very close second, and the combination of actions and words can't be beat. The words in this book belong to those who chose to act, and when repercussions were brought by the system of judges, prosecutors, and juries, these people chose to stand defiant.

Every one of these statements is imperfect, none of these people were/are heroes. Fortunately, we don't find inspiration in perfection, or heroics. We find inspiration in defiance.

Louise Michel

**LOUISE MICHEL**
**1871 & 1883**

LOUISE MICHEL WAS A FRENCH TEACHER AND anarchist. Born in 1830, Michel played a large role in the Paris Commune of 1871 as the head of the Montmartre Women's Vigilance Committee. At one point she was dissuaded from assassinating then President, Adolphe Thiers. Following the defeat of the Commune by the French government, Michel stood trial for her participation.

**JUDGE:** *You have heard the acts of which you are accused. What do you have to say in your defense?*

**MICHEL:** I don't want to defend myself. I don't want to be defended. I belong entirely to the social revolution, and I declare that I accept responsibility for all my actions. I accept it completely and without qualification. You accuse me of being involved in the killing of the generals? To that, I would answer yes, if I had found myself in Montmartre when they wanted to fire on the people; I would not have hesitated to fire on those who gave orders like those; but as soon as they were prisoners, I don't understand why they were shot, and I consider that act as one of remarkable cowardice!

As for the burning of Paris, yes, I participated in it. I wanted to put up a barrier of flames to the invaders of Versailles. I had no accomplices, I acted on my own.

You also say that I am an accomplice of the Commune! Of course I am, since the Commune wanted social revolution above all, and social revolution is my dearest wish. What is more, I am honored to be counted among the promoters of the Commune which, in any case, was absolutely not, absolutely not involved, as you well know, with the assassinations and the burnings: I attended all of the meetings at the Hôtel de Ville, and I affirm that there was never any question of assassination or burning. Do you want to know who the real culprits are? The police. Later, perhaps, light will shine on these events for which it is today so natural for us to blame all the partisans of social revolution.

One day, I proposed to [Théophile]Ferré an invasion of the Assembly. I wanted two victims, M. Thiers and myself, because I had made the sacrifice of my life, and I had decided to strike him down.

**JUDGE:** *In a proclamation, you said that every twenty-four hours a hostage should be shot?*

**MICHEL:** No, I only wanted to threaten. But why would I defend myself? I've already told you I refuse to do it. You are the men who are going to judge me; you're in front of me openly; you are men, and I, I am only a woman. And yet I look you straight in the face. I know very well that anything I tell you will not change my sentence in the slightest. Thus I have a single and final word before I sit down. We have never wanted anything but the triumph of the principles of the Revolution. I swear to it by our martyrs fallen on the field of Satory, by our martyrs I still acclaim openly here, and who will someday find an avenger.

Once again, I belong to you; do with me as you please. Take my life if you want it. I am not a woman who would dispute your wishes a single instant.

**JUDGE**: *You declare that you did not approve of the assassination of the generals, and yet people say that, when you learned of it, you shouted, "They shot them. It serves them right."*

**MICHEL**: Yes, I said that, I admit it. (I even recall that it was in the presence of citizens Le Moussu and Ferré.)

**JUDGE**: *So you approved of the assassination?*

**MICHEL**: If I may, what I said is not proof. The words that I spoke aimed at encouraging the revolutionary impulse.

**JUDGE**: *You also wrote in newspapers. In Le Cri du peuple, for example?*

**MICHEL**: Yes, I don't hide it.

**JUDGE**: *Every day these newspapers called for the confiscation of the clergy's property and other similar revolutionary measures. Such were your opinions, then?*

**MICHEL**: Of course. But note that we had never wanted to take those goods for ourselves. We thought only to give them to the people for their well-being.

**JUDGE**: *You called for the abolition of the magistrature?*

**MICHEL**: Because I always had in front of me examples of its errors. I remember the Lesurques affair and so many others.

**JUDGE:** *You acknowledge wanting to assassinate M. Thiers?*

**MICHEL:** Certainly...I said it already and I say it again.

**JUDGE:** *It seems that you wore various costumes during the Commune.*

**MICHEL:** I dressed as usual. I added only a red sash to my clothing.

**JUDGE:** *Didn't you wear men's clothing several times?*

**MICHEL:** A single time: it was March 18th. I dressed as a National Guardsman, so I wouldn't attract attention.

**JUDGE:** *Accused, do you have something to say in your defense?*

**MICHEL:** What I demand from you, you who claim to be the war council, who present yourselves as my judges, who do not hide like the Board of Pardons, from you who are military men and who judge me openly, it is the field of Satory that I demand, where our brothers have already fallen.

I must be removed from society; that's what you've been told to do. Well, the prosecutor is right! Since it seems that every heart that beats for freedom has no right to anything but a bit of lead, I demand my share! If you let me live, I will never cease crying out for vengeance, and I will denounce the assassins of the Board of Pardons to the vengeance of my brothers...

**JUDGE:** *I cannot let you speak if you continue in that tone.*

**MICHEL:** I'm finished...If you are not cowards, kill me...

FOLLOWING THIS, MICHEL WAS LED OUT OF THE COURT FOR deliberation. When she was brought back in, the court declared her guilty, and that her punishment would be deportation to the French penal colony of New Caldonia. (While 20,000 Communards were summarily executed, some 10,000 were deported to penal colonies.) When Michel was informed that she had twenty-four hours to appeal the verdict, she said "No! There is nothing to appeal. But I should prefer death!"

Once in New Caledonia, Michel befriended people of the indigenous Kanak population, siding with them in their revolt against colonial rule in 1878. In 1880, a general amnesty was declared for participants in the Paris Commune, and Michel returned to Paris, where she quickly returned to radical agitation.

In 1883, Michel led (along with Émile Pouget) a demonstration-turned-riot, for which she was again tried.

It's a real political proceeding that is being brought against us. It isn't us that they're prosecuting; it's the anarchist party that is being prosecuted through us. And that is the reason I had to refuse the offers to defend me made by Maître Balandreau and by our friend Laguerre who, not long ago, undertook to defend our friends from Lyon so warmly.

M. l'Avocat-général invoked the Law of 1871 against us. I will not bother to find out whether this Law of 1871 was made by the victors against the vanquished, against those they were crushing as a millstone crushes grain. That was the time when the National Guard was being hunted in the plains, when Gallifet was pursuing us into the catacombs, when the streets of Paris were piled on each side with corpses. There is one thing that surprises you, that appalls you, and it is a woman who dares to defend herself. People are not accustomed to seeing a woman who dares to think. People want, as Proudhon put it, to see a woman as either a housewife or a courtesan!

We carried the black flag because the demonstration was to be essentially peaceful, because it is the black flag of strikes, the flag of those who are hungry. Could we carry any other? The red flag is nailed up in the cemeteries and we only have the right to take it up when we can defend it. We cannot do that now. I've said it before and I repeat, it was essentially a peaceful demonstration.

I went to the demonstration. I had to go. Why was I arrested? I've traveled across Europe, saying that I do not recognize borders, saying that all of humanity has right to the heritage of humanity. And that heritage will not belong to us, accustomed to living in slavery, but to those who will have freedom and who will know how to enjoy it. That is how we defend the Republic. And when we are told that we are its enemies, we have only one response, that we have founded it upon thirty-five thousand of our corpses.

You talk of discipline, of soldiers firing on their officers. Do you believe, M. l'Avocat-général, that if, at Sedan, they had fired on their leaders who had betrayed them, they would not have done the right thing? We would not have had the rottenness of the Sedan.

M. l'Avocat-général talked a lot about soldiers. He praised those who brought the anarchist demonstrators back to their superiors. Are there a lot of officers, a lot of generals, who turned in the gifts from Chantilly and the manifestos of M. Bonaparte? I'm not putting d'Orléans or Bonaparte on trial; we only put their ideas on trial. M. Bonaparte was acquitted and we are prosecuted. I pardon those who commit the crime; I do not pardon the crime. Is it not the law of the powerful that dominates us? We want to replace it with rights, and that is our crime in its entirety!

Above the courts, beyond the twenty years of forced labor that you can sentence us to, beyond the eternity of forced labor if you want, I see the dawn of freedom and equality breaking.

Come on! You are fed up with it, you are disgusted with what is going on around you!...How can you calmly watch the proletariat suffer without end while others gorge themselves?

We knew that the demonstration at the Invalides would amount to nothing, yet it was necessary to go. Today we are in total destitution...We do not call this regime a republic. We would call a regime a republic where there is progress, where there is justice, where there is bread for all. But how does your Republic differ from the Empire? What is this talk of freedom of the courts when there is five years of forced labor in the end?

I did not want for the cry of the workers to be lost. You will do with me what you want. This isn't about me. It concerns a large part of France, a large part of the world, because people are becoming more and more anarchist. People are disgusted with the way power was used under M. Bonaparte. The people have already led many revolutions! Sedan rid us of Bonaparte. The people led one on March 18th. You will no doubt see more of them, and it is for that reason that we march full of confidence toward the future! Without authority resting in the hands of a single person, there will be light, there will be truth, and there will be justice. Authority given to one person is a crime. What we want is the authority of all. M. l'Avocat-général was accusing me of wanting to be a leader. I have too much pride for that. I cannot abase myself and being a leader is an abasement.

Here we are some distance from M. Moricet and his bakery, and I'm having trouble returning to those details. Must we speak of those crumbs handed out to some children? It's not bread that we needed; it's the bread of work we were demanding. How can you imagine reasonable men having a good time taking a few loaves of bread? That some kids have been gathering crumbs, that's fine, but it is tiresome to discuss such unserious things.

I would prefer to return to great ideas. Let young people work instead of going to cafés, and they will learn to fight to better the lives of the impoverished, to prepare the future. People recognize homelands only to make them a home for war. People recognize borders only to make of them an object to tamper with. The homeland, the family, we conceive them in a larger sense, spread wider. Those are our crimes.

We are in an era of anxiety. Everyone is seeking their own way. We say all the same: Come what may! Let freedom be realized! Let equality be achieved, and we will be happy!

The following day, when asked if she had more to say, she stated:

I wish only to say a word. This trial is a political trial. It is a political trial that you will have to judge. As for me, you have given me the role of the primary defendant. I accept it. Yes, I am the only one responsible. It was a long time ago that I sacrificed myself and that the standard was gone for what could be agreeable or disagreeable to me. I see only the Revolution! That alone is what I shall always serve. I salute the Revolution! May it rise up over men instead of rising up over ruins!

MICHEL WAS SENTENCED TO SIX YEARS OF SOLITARY CONFINEMENT. She was once again told that she had three days to appeal the sentence, and again, she replied "Never! You imitate all too well the Empire's magistrates."

After three years, Michel was released. But, just four years later, she was arrested again. The state attempted to commit her to an insane asylum, but she fled to London, where she started a school for the children of political refugees. She was active in the anarchist movement the rest of her life, agitating and writing. When she died in 1905, her funeral was attended by more than 100,000 people.

## PETER KROPOTKIN
## 1883

PETER KROPOTKIN WAS BORN A RUSSIAN prince, but declined this title to become a Russian anarchist. After escaping from a prison in St. Petersburg in a getaway horse-drawn buggy, Kropotkin fled Russia for England. He would also spend some years in Switzerland before being expelled in the aftermath of the assassination of Czar Alexander II, which he had nothing to do with. In 1883, he was arrested in Lyon, France, along with sixty-five other anarchists, all accused of belonging to the International Working Men's Association, which had split into anarchist and Marxist wings in 1872, and was criminalized and disbanded by a French law in the aftermath of the defeat of the Paris Commune. Kropotkin was sentenced to five years in prison, but was released in 1886. He died in 1921, after finding disappointment in the authoritarianism of the Russian Revolution. His funeral was the last legal gathering of anarchists in the USSR. Following is Kropotkin's speech to the court, as well as a manifesto that was read to the court in the name of all of the defendants.

I think, gentlemen, that like me you must have been struck by the weakness of the case brought against us. Are you in the presence of an international organisation? I may be excused from giving a reply, for the hearing is already well advanced, and the proof for this is still lacking. Anyway, it seems to me that the case fell at the same time that these words fell from the lips of the public prosecutor: "As long as there is a single anarchist in Lyon, I shall proceed against him with every law at my disposal." These are enough to show that the trial brought against us is a political trial, a class trial.

I said this trial was a class trial. I shall add that the people of a single country are divided by the establishment of the side of the bourgeoisie and the side of the workers. For the former—all rights, all privileges. For the latter—no freedom, no justice. The Law of 1872 indeed divides society into two classes, since it is aimed only at the International Working Men's Association. Is this not proved further by the right of the bourgeoisie to associate freely with foreigners without being prevented by law? Thus a number of French deputies were recently present at the unveiling of a monument raised to the Italian revolutionary Mazzini, who spent his whole life plotting against Austrian, French and Italian rulers. Have they been prosecuted? Have there not been meetings of Italian and French republicans in Paris for some time?

I have hesitated to defend myself before this trial which serves the interests of politics, of the moment, of a class. But there is someone above us who judges us: public opinion. That is who I am speaking to.

It would really be a very good thing if we could come and tell you that we belonged to the International. But we cannot, for that great workers' organisation has not existed in France since it was destroyed by the iniquitous Law of 1872. For my part, I should have been proud to tell you that I had joined this organisation, and I should have said so if this would have led to the release of the other accused. I shall never consider it a crime to say to workers of two continents: "Workers, when the bourgeoisie drive you to poverty, put aside your hatred, hold your hands out across the frontiers, be brothers!"

Ah, says the public prosecutor, we have no patriotism. Do you think my heart does not beat more quickly when a Russian song comes to my ears than when I hear a French one? But I love France, because I see this beautiful country as the home of revolutions, because I know that when it is conquered it is reaction which raises its head and freedom which is driven out. The public prosecutor has spoken to you of his patriotic sorrow when he saw his country invaded by the Prussian army. Let me remind him that at the time when France was devastated by war, there were some people who protested—they were German socialists.

A society which is divided into two distinct classes, one which produces but possesses nothing, the other which does not produce but possesses everything, is a society without morality, which is condemned by itself. A worker's labour represents an average of several thousand francs a year but his annual wage is often not a thousand francs. Next to this poverty is displayed the mad wastefulness of the bourgeois class. In what way can this shameful injustice of society be reformed? Science is powerless, and its work always benefits the leisured class. It was after all as a result of a violent expropriation that the bourgeoisie stripped land and wealth from the nobility and clergy.

I have been accused of being the father of anarchism. That is too much of an honour. It was Proudhon who first stated it in 1848, and Bakunin and other socialists who popularised it. We never stop working and studying in our groups but instead of coming and arguing with us you imprison and condemn us, because we defend those utopias—as you call our ideas—which will be realities tomorrow. The idea of anarchism has been stated and despite everything, despite the persecutions, has developed with astonishing speed. You can be sure that our conviction and imprisonment will bring us many more converts.

I believe the workers of two continents have their eyes on you, waiting with as much emotion as impatience for the judgement you are going to pronounce. If it is a conviction, they will say that the International was an excuse and that what you wanted to attack was the freedom to think and say what one thinks.

Do not stir up hatred. Repression has never achieved anything. Twice persecuted under the Empire, the International in 1870 more glorious and more powerful than before. Crushed in the streets of Paris beneath 35,000 corpses, after the Commune, socialism drew new life from the blood of its followers. Its ideas about property have been given an enormous circulation.

Believe me, gentlemen, the social revolution is near. It will break out within ten years. I live among the workers, and I am sure of it. Take inspiration from their ideas, join their ranks, and you will see that I am right. Let me tell you what I think. Do not stir up the hatred of the workers, for you will bring new misfortunes. You know that persecution is the best way to spread an idea. Is that what you want? Do you want a future of massacres for France? For, I repeat, ten years will not pass without a social revolution. What should you do in the presence of this revolution? Should you shrink from it and close your eyes, not wishing to hear or know anything about it? No, you should study the movement fairly, and look fairly to see whether by any chance we might be right.

I tell you, all of you who are listening, that the question is serious and inescapable. Perhaps you think it is rather bold to use such language in court. But if only two or three people are struck by the truth of my words and consider them as a salutary warning, I shall not have paid too much with a few years in prison for the satisfaction of having done my duty. If, by advising you to consider the certainty of a social revolution, I may prevent a few drops of blood from being spilt, I could die in prison and die happy.

However, if you persist in not listening, and if the bourgeoisie continues to subjugate, persecute and oppress the workers, the duty of every man of feeling is laid down in advance. I shall not fail in mine.

## MANIFESTO OF THE ANARCHISTS

What anarchism is, and what anarchists are, we shall try to explain: Anarchists, gentlemen, are citizens who, in an age when freedom of opinion is preached everywhere, have believed it to be their duty to call for unlimited freedom.

Yes, gentlemen, we are some thousand, some millions of workers, all over the world, who demand absolute freedom, nothing but freedom, the whole of freedom!

We want freedom—that is to say, we claim for every human being the right and the means to do whatever he pleases and only what he pleases, and to satisfy all his needs without any limit other than natural impossibilities and the needs of his neighbours, to be respected equally.

We want freedom, and we believe its existence to be incompatible with the existence of any kind of authority, whatever its origin and form may be, whether it is elected or imposed, monarchist or republican, whether it is inspired by divine right or by popular right, by holy oil[1] or by universal suffrage.

History is there to teach us that all governments are alike and equal. The best are the worst. There is more cynicism in some, more hypocrisy in others. In the end there is always the same behaviour, always the same intolerance. Even the most apparently liberal have in reserve, beneath the dust of legislative files, some nice little law on the International for use against troublesome opponents.

The evil, in other words, in the eyes of anarchists does not lie in one form of government rather than another. It lies in the

1   This was an anointing oil for the coronation of the kings of France. Its first recorded use was by Pope Innocent II for the anointing of Louis VII in 1131.

governmental idea itself, it lies in the principle of authority.

In short, the substitution in human relationships of a free contract which can be revised or cancelled in perpetuity, for administrative and legal tutelage, for imposed discipline—that is our ideal.

Anarchists therefore intend to teach the people to do without government, just as they are beginning to learn to do without God.

The people will similarly learn to do without property owners. The worst of tyrants, after all, is not the one who imprisons you but the one who starves you, not the one who holds on to your collar but the one who tightens up your belt.

There can be no liberty without equality. There is no liberty in a society where capital is monopolised in the hands of a minority which is growing smaller every day, and where nothing is shared equally—not even public education, although it is paid for by the contributions of all.

We believe that capital—the common inheritance of mankind, since it is the fruit of the co-operation of past and present generations—must be at the disposal of all in such a way that none may be excluded, and that in turn no one may get possession of a part to the detriment of the rest.

In a word, we want equality—real equality, as a corollary or rather as a prior condition of liberty. From each according to his abilities, to each according to his needs—that is what we sincerely and strenuously desire. That is what will come about, for no regulation can prevail against claims which are at the same time legitimate and necessary. That is why you want to condemn us to all kinds of hardship.

Scoundrels that we are, we demand bread for everyone, work for everyone, and for everyone independence and justice too!

**CLÉMENT DUVAL 1886**    CLÉMENT DUVAL WAS A FRENCH ANARCHIST, whose ideas were greatly influential on the French illegalists. On October 25, 1886, Duval broke into a Parisian mansion, accidentally set the house on fire, and made off with 15,000 francs. When he was arrested two weeks later, he resisted, stabbing the arresting officer several times. In a letter written to the anarchist newspaper *Le Révolté,* he said that *"Theft exists only through the exploitation of man by man...when Society refuses you the right to exist, you must take it...the policeman arrested me in the name of the Law, I struck him in the name of Liberty..."* After delivering his defense speech, he was declared guilty, sentenced to death, and dragged from the courtroom screaming *"Vive l'anarchie!"* His death sentence was later commuted to exile on the prison colony of Devil's Island in French Guiana. Duval attempted escape eighteen times, finally succeeding in 1901 at the age of 51, when he fled to New York City, and lived another 34 years amongst the Italian immigrant anarchist community there.

While I do not recognize your right to pose to me the questions that you have, I have responded to you as the accused.

Now, you are the ones that I am accusing. I do not pretend to defend myself. To what end would this serve me, in front of those as well armed as you, having soldiers, cannons, police, and finally an army of mercenaries as your henchmen?

Let's be logical, you are in power, taking advantage of it, and if you still need the head of yet another anarchist, take it, and when our day comes we will take this into account, and I have the firm hope that on that day the anarchists will rise to the occasion. They will be without pity, because never will they reach the number of your victims.

It is not only you who I am addressing, but to all of this selfish, cruel, corrupt society, where on one side we see an orgy and on the other misery!

You have accused me of theft, as if a worker that has nothing could be a thief.

No, theft exists only in the exploitation of man by man, in a word by those who live at the expense of the working class. It was not a theft that I committed, but a just restitution made in the name of humanity, this money was to serve for making revolutionary propaganda, through writing and by the deed. To make newspapers and leaflets to show people the truth; it has been a long time that they have been deceived. To show the cure to those who are ill.

I busy myself with chemistry and prepare what is needed for the day of battle, the day when the workers, conscious, will leave their torpor, their slump. Because it is time that this diabolic machination of the old world disappear, to give place to institutions where all will find a fate that is more fair, which does not exist but within anarchist communism.

Because anarchy is the negation of all authority.

And anarchy is the biggest social wound, because man is not free, and one must become free to do all that one wants, as long as one does not infringe upon the liberty of their fellow—for then one would become a despot in turn.

In communism, man gives to society according to his skills and strengths, and should receive according to his needs. Men group themselves, find each other according to their character, their skills, their affinities, taking as an example the group which functions the best, away from vanity, foolish pride, not seeking to do better than one's comrade for one can do better for one's self.

Out of this will come the useful masterpieces, people's intelligence no longer reduced to nothing but capital, because men would be able to evolve freely, no longer under the despotic yoke of authority, of individual property. And these groups can mutually exchange their products, unhindered.

Learning, and feeling good about governing themselves, they will federate and will be nothing more than a big family of workers associated together for the happiness of all—one for all, all for one—knowing only a single law: the law of solidarity and reciprocity.

No more gold, base metal for which I am here and which I despise. Base metal, the cause of all the evils and vices that afflict humanity. Base metal, with which men's conscience is bought!

With anarchist communism, there is no more exploitation of man by man, no more of these managers of sweat, no more salesmen with a mercantile spirit, rapacious, selfish, poisoning, falsifying their products and their commodities, thereby bringing the degradation of mankind.

You cannot deny this, because you see this all the way to the toy salesmen, who already poison with these toys the poor little creatures who are barely born.

And these factories, where they play with the workers lives with an unparalleled shamelessness, like in the factories of white lead where in only a few months the workers find themselves paralyzed and soon dead, or in the tinsmiths who in little time become bald, crippled, weakened in the bones and die in agony!

There are scientists who know that they can replace these unhealthy products with innocuous ones. The doctors who see these unfortunates twist in such agony and who leave things to continue, they allow these crimes against humanity to happen. Even better, they decorate the heads of the factories, and they award them honorary awards in memory of the service they have given to industry and humanity.

And how many of these unhealthy industries are there? The number would be too large to count them all, not to mention the foul and unhealthy capitalist prisons where the worker, imprisoned for ten or twelve hours is obligated, for the sake of conserving his family's bread, to incur the vexations, the humiliation of an insolent convict, missing only the whip for us all to recall the heyday of ancient slavery and medieval serfdom.

And the unfortunate miners, imprisoned five or six hundred feet underground, seeing the light of day no more than once a week and when, tired of so much misery and suffering, they lift their heads to reclaim their right to sunlight and to the banquet of life: quickly the army is in the countryside at the service of the exploiters, and we shoot this scoundrel! The proof doesn't default.

And the exploitation of man by man is nothing compared to that experienced by women. Nature is already thankless in this regard, to make them sick fifteen days of the month, but we hardly take this into account: flesh of profit, flesh for fun, this is the fate of women. How many young girls arrive from the countryside, full of strength and health, only to be enclosed in the workshops, in rooms where there is room for four and they are fifteen, twenty, without air, breathing nothing but pollution: hardships they are forced to self-impose. After six months they are anemic. From there the sickness, weakness, and dislike of work that is not even sufficient to meet their needs drives these unfortunates to prostitution.

What does society do for these victims? It rejects them from her breast, like the leper, puts them on the map, enrolls them with the police, and makes informers of their lovers.

And do you think the workers, with noble and generous sentiments, can see this picture of the human life unfurling constantly before their eyes without being revolted? He who feels all these effects, who is constantly a victim of them, morally, physically, and materially: he who is taken at twenty-years old to pay his taxes in blood, cannon fodder to defend the property and privileges of his masters: and if he returns from this butchery, he returns maimed or with a sickness that renders him half crippled, making him go from hospital to hospital serving therefore as experimental flesh for these gentlemen of science. I know what I speak of, I who have returned from the carnage with two wounds and rheumatism, a sickness that has given me four years in the hospital and which prevents me from working six months of the year. As an incentive, if you do not have the courage to give them my head as they ask, I will die in prison.

And these crimes are committed in broad daylight, after being plotted in the corridors of the government, under the influence of a clique, or the caprice of a woman, while shouting over the rooftops: The people are sovereign, The Nation is sovereign, and under the buzz words of patronage—Glory, Honor, Homeland, as if there were several homelands between all beings living on the same planet.

*No!* The anarchists have but one party, and that is humanity.

It is also, in the name of civilization that exists these distant expeditions where thousands of men are killed with a savage ferocity. It is in the name of civilization that we plunder, that we burn, that we massacre an entire people who demand nothing [more] than to live peacefully in their homes. And these crimes are committed with impunity because the law doesn't cover this type of theft and armed robbery, au contraire: We award medals to those who have led all this carnage, medals to the mercenaries who have taken part, in memory of their good deeds, and these unconscious ones are proud to wear this insignia which is nothing but a diploma of assassination.

But on the other hand, the law severely punishes the worker to whom society refuses the right to exist and who has the courage to take what is necessary, which he lacks, where there is superfluous amounts. Oh! And then this one is treated like a thief, brought before the court and finally returns to end his days in prison.

*Voila!* The logic of our current society.

Ah well, this is the crime that I am here for: for not recognizing the right of these people to die of plenty while the producers, the creators of all social wealth, starve. Yes, I am the enemy of individual property and it has been a long time that I have said, along with Proudhon, that property is theft.

In effect, how does one acquire property, if not through theft, by exploiting one's fellows, giving three francs to the exploited for a job which will bring back ten for the exploiter? And the little exploiters don't do it any differently. Evidence: I have seen my companion do work as the second hand, two little detached pieces of lace and pearls, for which she was paid seven and a half centimes a piece. Fifteen days later, doing the same work as the first hand, he was paid fifty five centimes a piece.

So do you think that a conscious worker could be so stupid that one the day to pay the rent, to give back to the same exploiter-owner a part of his salary which had been given to him? And he will see his wife and children forced to deprive themselves of things most necessary for life, while the idle, with this money, goes to the stock exchange or somewhere else to speculate, play the market on the misery of the people, or wallow in some fashionable boudoir in the arms of an unwell girl, who to live is forced to give her flesh to others for pleasure, despite the disgust that it inspires in her.

As I do not want myself to be made an accomplice of the likes of these dishonorables, this is why I do not pay rent (for which you reproach me), not wanting myself to be robbed by this thief, this vulture that we call an owner, and this is why I had received bad references in the different areas that I have lived. Good references are only given for the vile and the groveling, for those who have no backbone.

Because the law is in all things the accomplice of those who own, the throw away the anathema at the workers who lift their heads proudly, who retain their dignity by revolting against abuse, injustices, against the monsters who make up the owning class.

But, it has been a long time since I have reckoned with anything but my conscience, mocking the fools and the wicked, feeling certain that I have the esteem of men of heart who have known me closely. This is why I am telling you: you are not condemning me as a thief, but as a conscious worker, who does not consider oneself to be a beast of burden, taxable and thanklessly exploited, and who recognizes the undeniable right that nature gives to all human beings: the right to existence. And if society refuses us this right, we must take it with unshaking hands (which would be a cowardice in a society where all abounds, where everything is in abundance, where what should be a source of wellbeing is nothing more than a source of misery)... Why? Because everything is monopolized by a handful of idlers who burst from indigestion while the workers are continually searching for a loaf of bread.

*No!* I am not a robber but one who has been robbed, someone who brings justice, who says that everything belongs to everyone, and that it is this clear logic of the anarchist idea, which makes your legs tremble.

No, I am not a thief but a sincere revolutionary, who has

the courage of his convictions and who is devoted to his cause. Within the current society, where money is the nerve of war, I would do all that is within my power to procure it to serve this noble and just cause which would purge humanity of all of the tyrannies, the persecutions that it has suffered so cruelly.

Ah! I have only one regret, which is to have fallen too early into your hands, this preventing me from satisfying an implacable hatred, a thirst for vengeance that I have vowed upon so infamous a society.

But what consoles me is that there are combatants that remain, because despite all the persecution, the anarchist idea has germinated, and the theoretical revolution is ending, being quickly replaced by the practice of action. Oh, then, that day—rotten society, governments, magistrates, exploiters of all kinds, you have lived!

*Long live social revolution, vive l'anarchie!*

**LOUIS LÉVEILLÉ 1891**

On May Day of 1891, a few dozen anarchists held a demonstration in Clichy, France. When police tried to stop the demonstration, the anarchists fought back, gunfire going in both directions. In the melee, Louis Léveillé was shot in the leg, and arrested along with Charles Auguste Dardare and Henry Louis Decamps. At trial (known as the Clichy Affair), Decamps declared "My head? We can cut it off. I will deliver it: I will carry it proud and straight on to the scaffold. One anarchist head more or less will not prevent our propaganda." Of the three, only Léveillé was acquitted, while Decamps and Dardare each got five and three years in prison respectively. Léveillé declared the following.

---

I asked my comrade and friend, Sébastien Faure, to present my defense. Even though the law, by special arrangement, allows the accused to choose his defender, either a relative or friend outside the profession of lawyers, Your Honor has clearly refused my request on this matter.

First of all I protest against this disrespect of the law committed by those very men who are responsible for applying it within these walls and yet do not respect it.

I regret that Sébastien Faure is not in the defense box, first because I know better than anyone else that he is the most likely to help me here; and then since the matter is not what the Members of the Jury are used to examining everyday, it will take a comrade, a partner, an anarchist to give or convey to these arguments the style they deserve; and finally because with the persuasive, lively and sincere eloquence that characterizes the apostles of our Idea, Sébastien Faure could make you understand the motives that have brought me before you and he could explain to you the whys and wherefores of this struggle that my friends and I have supported against the local and national police who have assaulted us. And I am sure, Sirs, that your verdict would be for acquittal.

I am forced to express at the beginning of my defense these regrets of mine and my firm objection.

If, in the first days after my arrest and in the course of my trial, I denied firing a shot, it is not, sirs, because I wanted to shirk the responsibility of my actions. But convinced that if absolutely reliable witnesses did not come forward, I would be released and figuring that when up against the representatives of the authority imprisoning me all ends are fair to be free, I had, for an instant, hope.

But today, I have declared and I categorically declare that I fired on those who attacked me. I have done my duty like my friends Decamp and Dardare. I want to be sentenced or acquitted with them. If you find them guilty, I am guilty, too. And I will take my part of the responsibility full and entire.

I will not try to arouse your anger by telling you how they treated us. Suffice it to say, sirs, that after being shot in the thigh, devoured by fever and in serious pain, when I asked for water to clean my wound, they answered me with their boots and pistol

Clichy, May 1, 1891

butts. Suffice it to say that this painful agony lasted for six days and remained without care until May 20, that is for twenty days in all. And yet, sirs, in times of war, even when the most savage instincts have free rein, it is an absolute rule that the wounded who have fallen into enemy hands will be cared for and the prisoners respected. But for the police, we are worse than enemies because we are revolutionaries—we are *anarchists*.

And so it should be no surprise that the prosecution is seeking the death penalty for us. And why? Because, being the determined adversaries of the Authority that starves, humiliates, imprisons and kills, we want Anarchy to triumph. Anarchy that they have always represented as a doctrine of hatred and violence but that is, in reality, a doctrine of peace, fraternity and love, seeing that the goal of Anarchy is to substitute the solidarity of individual interests for their opposition and to replace competition (the source of all dualism, of all animosity and of all social crimes) with universal association and harmony.

The people who stand most vehemently against anarchist theories are those who understand them the least. Anarchy, which in the present state of things is not and cannot be but a negation of the entire authoritarian system, is not and cannot be, during a struggle, but the practice of disobedience, insubordination and defiance—in a word, revolt.

As such, the anarchist idea is as old as the principle of authority because from the day when a man claimed he commanded other men, these men more or less refused to obey. But just as ignorance created the gods and gave birth to governmental systems, so this same ignorance kept humans from shaking off the yoke and clearly seeing their rights.

Moreover, it was bound to happen that being thrown on a planet with inexhaustible treasures in its belly, but not knowing how to dig and make the most of it, humans, faced with the difficulties of feeding themselves, of protecting themselves against bad weather and of moving freely, argued and fought and killed each other to get what their desires, needs, and aspirations demanded.

The recognition of this perpetual "struggle for life" might make you think that these conflicts, rivalries and battles are inevitable, that they have always existed and that they will continue until the end of history. But ignorance, that evil of primitive ages, has been gradually reduced by the knowledge accumulated over the centuries. Humanity has been steadily enriched in wonderful ways; the conquests of the human mind have multiplied; the horizon has expanded beyond measure; the elements tamed by man have become his most diligent, most docile and most disinterested collaborators; labor, supported by Science, has made extraordinary underground riches spring forth; farming, expertly developed, has covered the ground with wonderful crops, savory fruits, sweet-scented flowers and hardy trees; floods have been averted, epidemics victoriously battled; natural evils have been almost wiped out!

And in the heart of this fertile, beautiful, luxuriant earth, some men, who once stood side by side with others to reach their goals, have been stupid enough to keep wanting to grab everything; and others stupid enough to accept being despoiled. The grabbers are scandalously becoming richer and richer and fewer and fewer while the family of disinherited are becoming poorer and poorer and more and more numerous. How is it that these millions and millions of poor do not get any payback from this handful of billionaires?

It is not too hard to answer this question. This comes from:

First, every kind of prejudice carefully maintained by the privileged in the brains of the masses; these prejudices are the government, laws, property, religion, country, family, etc. This is a moral restraint.

Second, the system of repression that dishonors the land: judges, police, soldiers, prison guards—there is your physical restraint.

To sum up, I'll say that the evil comes from the law that, being made by those in power, has no other purpose but to justify their imposture, to consecrate their depredation and to guarantee their impunity; the law that requires a governmental system which logically drags behind it the coercive and repressive forces I just mentioned.

Everyone is aware these truths. To such a point that they are starting to wonder today if a government is really necessary. While the partisans of all authoritative systems say "yes," the anarchists alone say "no." And at the end of this 19th century, the anarchist concept is summed up in these three words that have the power of terrifying some and making others smile in disbelief: "No more government."

Yes, no more government.

Everything is there because from the day that the government (and I mean by this *every* governmental system, whatever the form and whatever its name), from the day, then, that every government disappears, the written laws and the codes will have no more reason to exist, seeing that they will no longer rely on any force to be feared and respected. At the same time, natural law will easily take the place of artificial laws because, don't forget, sirs, Anarchy is free play in the humanity of natural laws or, more precisely, (since I want to avoid this word "law") of the natural forces that regulate the entire Universe.

No more Codes! No more judges! No more police! No more soldiers! No more priests! No more leaders! In a word, no more governments!

Such is our watchword! Such is our rallying cry! Such is the slogan of Anarchy fighting against the old social order.

And why a government? Ask individually each of the 500 people assembled here.

A strange thing. Recognizing that it is not the government that cultivates the land, sews clothes, kneads bread, builds houses, mines coal, fabricates machines, writes books and pushes knowledge in new directions, each will answer that *for him* a government is useless, that he does not feel the need. And grouped together, assembled here, when I come to say that this useless machinery is harmful, that it sucks out all our energy, costs too much to maintain (and you know as well as I do what the cost of governmental machinery is!) and therefore this harmful machinery should be done away with, you rear up under the whiplash of this simple statement!

Why is that? Because for centuries they have said over and over again, "A government is necessary." And your fathers believed it and without even thinking, you believe it, too.

If you open any dictionary to the letter A and look up the word Anarchy, you will see the following definition: "Chaos, upheaval, absence of order and harmony." Is this the meaning of Anarchy? It comes from two Greek words: Alpha privative, A, meaning "absence of" and Arke which means "power." So that according to official knowledge, absence of order is synonymous with absence of power and we should conclude that there is no order without authority and where there is no government, there can only be disorder.

Ah! How easy it would be for me to take this error in hand and, with my eyes open not only on the past but on the present as well, to prove that this age of ours is living under a regime of excessive governmental centralization but our generation is running around in appalling disorder.

Allow me, briefly, in a few quick images, to paint you a picture of Modern Society.

On the top:

Priests trafficking religious sacraments and ceremonies; bureaucrats bowing their heads but ripping off and running off with the cash; military officers selling so-called national defense secrets to the enemy; writers directing their thoughts to glorify injustice, poets idealizing the ugly, artists *apotheosizing* the iniquitous, as long as their depravity lands them a cushy chair at the Academy, a seat at the Institute, or some entitlements... an income.

Lying salesmen cheating on the weight, quality and provenance of their merchandise; industrialists adulterating their products; speculators fishing for billions in the inexhaustible Ocean of human stupidity.

Politicians, thirsting for domination, banking on the ignorance of some and the good faith of others; pencil pushers, so-called journalists, prostituting their pens with an indifference that has no equal except in the foolishness of the readers.

On the bottom:

Home builders without homes, garment workers without clothes, bakers without bread, billions of producers suffering unemployment and therefore hunger; crowds of people wandering around, all over the place, in search of a bridge to build, a tunnel to construct, a hole to dig; families piled up in slums; fifteen-year old girls, in order to eat, forced to put up with the foul gropings of old men and the lewd assaults of young bourgeoisie.

Blind masses, who seem totally unfit to recognize their dignity; this rabble rushing after a minister who exploits them, and lavishing ridiculous praise on him; crowds gathering at a station before a monarch, a son, brother, or cousin of the coming king; and in the intoxication of national celebrations, in the numbing fanfares and whirling public balls, people willingly forget that yesterday they were dying in misery and slavery and tomorrow they will perish in servitude and hardship.

Such is the desperate picture that our present humanity offers. That is the order that the most *governmentalized* of Societies offers you.

And while the colors are very dark indeed, they are not painted on for fun; there is depravity, shame, atrocity and torture that no human language can describe.

But at the heart of this corruption that is eating away at the powerful and of this servility that dishonors the weak, at the heart of this hypocritical cynicism that characterizes the haughty and of the incredible naivety in which the lowly perish, in the midst of the insolence that the "upper classes" flaunt and of the fawning of the "lower classes," in the midst of the savage greed of the robbers and of the unfathomable apathy of the robbed, between the wolves of power, religion and wealth and the sheep of work, poverty and servitude, there are a handful of brave men standing tall, a phalanx that has not been contaminated by the arrogance of the haughty or the platitudes of the humble.

Yesterday a half a handful; today an army; tomorrow a numberless crowd; they follow the Truth; they care no more about the fearful tittering of the rich than they do about the dreary indifference of the poor.

To the powerful they say:

"You reign only through ignorance and fear. You are the degenerate heirs of barbarians, tyrants and criminals.

"Who maintains you in your idle lives? Your victims!

"Who protects you and defends you against the enemies from within and without? O bitter irony—Your victims!

"Who elects you into public office? Once again, your victims!

"And their ignorance, so carefully maintained by you, not only does not see these disturbing inconsistencies, but it turns it into resignation, respect, almost veneration.

"But we will unmask you without pity and we will expose your hideous faces, you butchers, where we can see the hypocrisy, avarice, pride and cowardice."

And what do these same men say to the lowly, the exploited, the enslaved?

Listen:

"O you who are born in a cradle of straw, who grow up in the claws of misery and live condemned to hard labor and the premature old age of scapegoats, don't despair.

"Proletariat, grandsons of ancient slaves, sons of medieval serfs, know that your misery is not hopeless.

"All of you who make up this enslaved humanity whose wounded feet have left bloody traces in its human wake for too many centuries now, trust in the future.

"In rags, in pain, with empty stomachs, barefoot, exploited, wounded, disinherited, you are drained a little more every day by the power and prestige of your masters but every day your battalions are becoming stronger and stronger.

"Lift up your hearts and your heads! Know your rights! Understand that every man is equal to every other man. It is wrong that some have rights to exercise and others duties to fulfill. Refuse to obey and no one will think of commanding you.

"At last, raise up your dignity.

"Let the spirit of revolt grow in you and with Freedom you will become happy!"

That, sirs, is what anarchists are. Such is their language and such is ours.

I conclude:

We are guilty if by awaking the sense of dignity among our comrades, we fail to do so in ourselves.

Criminals, yes, we will be criminals if by calling men to revolt, we bow before the threats and submit to the orders of the representatives of authority.

Cowards, the worst of cowards if arousing the courage of our partners in the fight and encouraging them to be brave, we do not defend our life and liberty when they are in danger.

That is why I had to do what I did, we had to do what we did (my friends, I know, think the same as me). And we have no regrets.

If you condemn me, my convictions will remain unshakable.

There will be one more anarchist in prison, but one hundred more on the streets. And our example will be followed. It will be the starting point of revolts that will multiply, that will become more and more collective, until the universal Revolution introduces into the everyday world the ideas for which I live, for which I suffer with a certain joy, for which I am ready, like all anarchists, to shed my blood if necessary, without swaggering or staggering, until not a drop is left.

**RAVACHOL 1892**  Ravachol was a French anarchist and accordionist. Following the sentencing of two anarchists to prison during the Clichy Affair, Ravachol took revenge against the French authorities by bombing the homes of two of the judges that had conducted the trial. He received a life sentence at the trial for these bombings, neither of which resulted in injury or death, and then had to face trial for a number of murders, in which he was found guilty and sentenced to death by guillotine. He attempted to read the following statement at trial, but was cut off by the judge before getting more than a few words in.

---

If I speak, it's not to defend myself for the acts of which I'm accused, for it is society alone that is responsible, since by its organization it sets man in a continual struggle of one against the other. In fact, don't we see today, in all classes and all positions, people who desire, I won't say the death, because that doesn't sound good, but the ill fortune of their fellows if they can gain advantages from this? For example, doesn't a boss hope to see a competitor die? And don't all businessmen reciprocally hope to be the only one to enjoy the advantages that their occupations bring? In order to obtain employment, doesn't the unemployed worker hope that for some reason or another someone who does have a job will be thrown out of his workplace. Well then, in a society where such things occur, there's no reason to be surprised about the kind of acts for which I'm blamed, which are nothing but the logical consequence of the struggle for existence that men carry on who are obliged to use every means available in order to live. And since it's every man for himself, isn't he who is in need reduced to thinking: "Well, since that's the way things are, when I'm hungry I have no reason to hesitate about using the means at my disposal, even at the risk of causing victims! Bosses, when they fire workers, do they worry whether or not they're going to die of hunger? Do those who have a surplus worry if there are those who lack the basic necessities?"

There are some who give assistance, but they are powerless to relieve all those in need who will either die prematurely because of privations of various kinds, or voluntarily by suicides of all kinds, in order to put an end to a miserable existence and to not have to put up with the rigors of hunger, with countless shames and humiliations, and who are without hope of ever seeing them end. Thus there are the Hayem and Souhain families, who killed their children so as not to see them suffer any longer, and all the women who, in fear of not being able to feed a child, don't hesitate to destroy in their wombs the fruit of their love.

And all these things happen in the midst of an abundance of all sorts of products. We could understand if these things happened in a country where products are rare, where there is famine. But in France, where abundance reigns, where butcher shops are loaded with meat, bakeries with bread, where clothing and shoes are piled up in stores, where there are unoccupied lodgings! How can anyone accept that everything is for the best in a society when the contrary can be seen so clearly? There are many people who will feel sorry for the victims, but who'll tell you they can't do anything about it. Let everyone scrape by as he can! What can he who lacks the necessities when he's working do when he loses his job? He has only to let himself die of hunger. Then people will throw a few pious words on his corpse. This is what I wanted to leave to others. I preferred to make of myself a trafficker in contraband, a counterfeiter, a murderer, and an assassin. I could have begged, but it's degrading and cowardly and even punished by your laws, which make poverty a crime. If all those in need, instead of waiting took, wherever and by whatever means, the self-satisfied would perhaps understand a bit more quickly that it's dangerous to want to consecrate the existing social state, where worry is permanent and life threatened at every moment.

We can immediately see that the anarchists are right when they say that in order to have moral and physical peace the causes that give rise to crime and criminals must be destroyed. We won't achieve these goals by suppressing the man who, rather than die a slow death caused by the privations he had and will have to put up with without any hope of ever seeing them end, prefers—if he has the least bit of energy—to violently take what can ensure his well-being, even at the risk of death, which would only put an end to his sufferings.

So that is why I committed the acts of which I am accused, and which are nothing but the logical consequence of the barbaric state of a society that does nothing but increase the rigor of the laws that pursue the effects without ever touching the causes. It is said that you must be cruel to kill your fellow man, but those who say this don't see that you resolve to do this only to avoid the same fate.

In the same way you, gentlemen of the jury, will doubtless sentence me to death, because you think it is necessary and that my death will be a source of satisfaction for you who hate to see human blood flow. But when you think it is useful to have it flow in order to ensure the security of your existence you hesitate no more than I do, but with this difference: you do it without running any risk, while I, on the other hand, acted at the risk of my very life.

Well, *messieurs*, there are no more criminals to judge, but the causes of crime to do away with! In creating the articles of the Criminal Code, the legislators forgot that they didn't attack the causes, but only the effects, and so they don't in any way destroy crime. In truth, the causes continuing to exist, the effects will necessarily flow from them. There will always be criminals, for today you destroy one, but tomorrow ten will be born.

What, then, is needed? Destroy poverty, that seed of crime, by assuring everyone the satisfaction of their needs! How difficult this is to realize! All that is needed is to establish society on a new basis, where everything will be held in common and where each, producing according to his abilities and his strength, could consume according to his needs. Then and only then will we no longer see people such as the hermit of Notre-Dame-de-Grâce and others, begging for a coin whose victims and slaves they become! We will no longer see women surrendering their charms, like a common piece of merchandise, in exchange for this same coins, that often prevents us from recognizing whether or not affection is sincere. We will no longer see men such as Pranzini, Prado, Berland, Anastay,[1] and others who kill in order to have this same metal. This shows that the cause of all crimes is always the same, and you have to be foolish not to see this.

Yes, I repeat it: it is society that makes criminals and you, gentlemen of the jury, instead of striking you should
use your intelligence and your strength to transform society.

---

1   Famous criminals of the late 1880s and early 1890s. All were executed.

In one fell swoop you'll suppress all crime. And your work, in attacking causes, will be greater and more fruitful than your justice, which belittles itself in punishing its effects.

I am nothing but an uneducated worker; but because I have lived the life of the poor, I feel more than a rich bourgeois does the iniquity of your repressive laws. What gives you the right to kill or lock up a man who, put on earth with the need to live, found himself obliged to take that which he lacks in order to feed himself?

I worked to live and to provide for my family; as long as neither I nor my family suffered too much, I remained what you call honest. Then work became scarce, and with unemployment came hunger. It is only then that the great law of nature, that imperious voice that accepts no reply, the instinct of preservation, forced me to commit some of the crimes and misdemeanors of which I am accused and of which I admit I am the author.

Judge me, gentlemen of the jury, but if you have understood me, while judging me judge all the unfortunate who poverty, combined with natural pride, made criminals, and who wealth or ease would have made honest men.

'An intelligent society would have made of them men like any other!

Ravachol

**GEORGES ETIÉVANT 1892**

GEORGES ETIÉVANT WAS A FRENCH INDIVIDU-alist anarchist typographer born in Paris in 1865. In 1892 he was tried for stealing dynamite, which was subsequently used in attacks carried out by Ravachol. He was found guilty and sentenced to five years in prison. Upon release he began writing for the long running anarchist periodical, *Le Libertaire*. In 1898 he was tried in absentia for the publishing of an article in *Le Libertaire* titled "Le lapin et le chasseur" (The Rabbit and the Hunter). Though he wasn't present, he was sentenced to two years in prison. Eventually a pair of cops found him in the night, both of whom were stabbed by Etiévant, but restrained him. Upon arrival at the police station, Etiévant shot a third cop with his gun that hadn't been found by the first pair. He was then tried, found guilty, and sentenced to death. Ultimately his death sentence was commuted to life at forced labor in the French prison colony in Guiana where he died just two years later. The following speech was written for his first trial, though the judge refused to let him read it.

I wish to make a few remarks as to my position here at the bar on trial, and to yours, gentlemen of the jury, as my judges. I want to say that our ideas are so different that we should at least make the attempt to comprehend the forces that have influenced and controlled us both. We are not born into the world with any preconceptions; no ideas are innate in us. They came to us by means of our senses, through the environment in which we lived.

So true is this, that if we are devoid of a sense we cannot form any conception of the sensations resulting in that sense. For instance, a person blind from birth can have no idea of the variety of color, because he is devoid of the faculty required for perceiving the color of objects. Besides, according to the abilities with which we are born, we posses, in a greater or less degree, in one line of thought or another, a power of assimilation arising from the greater or less degree of receptivity which we possess on that subject. Thus, for instance, some learn with ease mathematics, whilst others show a great aptitude for languages. This power of assimilation which we possess can be developed in each of us to an extent varying ad infinitum, by means of the multiplicity of analogous sensations which we receive.

But just as, if we use our arms almost exclusively, they will acquire greater strength to the detriment of our other limbs or sections of our body, they will become more apt to fulfill their office in proportion as our other limbs become less so, even so the more out power of assimilation exercises itself in consequence of the multiplicity of analogous sensations produced by one line of thought, all the more, relatively to the whole of our faculties, shall we resist the assimilation of ideas derived from an adverse line of thought. Thus it is that, if we have come to consider one sort of thing or idea true and good, we shall be shocked at all contrary ideas and oppose a great power of resistance to their assimilation, although to another they may appear so natural and so just that we cannot in good faith understand how one can think otherwise. Every day we see examples of this, and I do not think any one will seriously deny its truth. This fact once formulated and admitted, as each act if the result of one or several ideas, it becomes evident that in order to judge a man, in order to understand the responsibility of the individual in the accomplishment of a deed, we must be able to know each of the sensations which have led to the accomplishment of that deed, appreciate their intensity, know the power of assimilation or force of resistance which each of them has encountered in him, as well as the time during which he has been under the influence first of each of them, then of several, and last of all.

Now who can give you the faculty of perceiving and feeling what others perceive and feel or have perceived and felt? How can you judge an individual if you can not know precisely the causes which have determined his act? And how can you get to know all these causes as well as their relationship to each other, if you cannot penetrate the hidden workings of his brain and identify yourself with him so as to know perfectly his inner self? But in order to do that it would be necessary to understand his disposition better than one often understands one's own, much more than this; it would be necessary to have a similar disposition, to subject oneself to the same influences, to live in the same environment for the same period, for that would be the only way to become aware of the number and strength of the influences of that environment when compared with the power of assimilation which those influences have encountered in the individual.

It is thus impossible to judge our fellow creatures, as it is impossible for us to know precisely the influences which they obey and the strength of the sensations which determine their acts when compared with their power of assimilation or their forces of resistance. But if this impossibility did not exist we should, at the most, only be able to appreciate exactly the various influences which they obeyed, their mutual relationship, the greater or lesser power of submitting themselves to these influences; but, for all that, we should not be able to judge of their responsibility in the accomplishment of an act, for this good and great reason—that responsibility does not exist.

To understand well the non-existence of responsibility it suffices to consider the various intellectual faculties displayed in man. For responsibility to exist it would be necessary that the will should determine the sensations, just as these determine the thought and that determines the act. But, on the contrary, it is the sensations which determine the will, which give rise to it in us, and which direct it. For will is only the desire which we have to accomplish something destined to satisfy one of our needs, that is to say, to obtain a pleasurable sensation, to avoid a painful sensation; consequently we must feel or have felt these sensations in order that *will* may rise in us. And will, created in us by the sensations, can only be changed by new sensations; that is to say, it can only take a new direction, pursue a different object, if new sensations give rise in us to a new line of thought or modify our former line of thought. This has been recognized in all ages; you yourselves tacitly acknowledge it; for, after all, do you not hear pleaded before you the case for the prosecution and the defense, that new sensations, reaching you through the sense of hearing, can give rise in you to a will to act in one way or another, or modify your former will? But as I said in the beginning, if one is accustomed, in consequence of a long succession of analogous sensations, to consider one idea good and just, all contrary ideas will shock us, and we shall present a great force of resistance of the assimilation of them.

It is for this reason that old people adopt with difficulty new ideas because, in the course of their existence, they have been subjected to a number of sensations arising from the environment in which they have lived, which have led them to consider as good ideas those which are in accordance with the generally accepted idea of right and wrong prevailing in that environment. It is for this same reason that the conception of justice and injustice has constantly varied in the course of centuries, that today it varies greatly in different countries, in different nations, and even in different men; and, as these diverse conceptions can only be *relatively* good and just, we must conclude that a great portion, if not the whole, of mankind are still at fault in this subject. This also explains to us why an argument which will convince one man will leave another unmoved.

But, whichever happens, he who is struck by an argument will be unable to prevent his will being influenced by it in some direction; and he whom the argument has left unmoved will be unable to prevent his will from remaining in the same condition as before; consequently, the one will be unable to prevent himself from acting in one way, the other in a contrary way—unless new sensations should intervene to modify their will.

Although it may sound like a paradox we perform no act, good or bad, no matter how insignificant it may be, which we are not forced to perform, since every act is the result of the relationship which exists between one or more sensations arising from the environment in which we live and the greater or lesser power of assimilation which they may encounter in us. Then, since we cannot be responsible for the greater or lesser power of assimilation which we possess with regard to some order of sensations, not for the existence or non-existence of influences arising from the environment in which we live and for the sensations which result from it, any more than for their relationship to each other or for our greater or lesser respective faculty or force of resistance; neither can we be responsible for the result of this relationship, since it is not only independent of our will but, in fact, determines our will. Thus any judicial act is impossible, and punishment and reward are alike unjust, however slight they may be, and however great may be the good or evil of the deed.

One cannot thus judge men or even their acts without a sufficient criterion, and this criterion does not exist; at any rate it cannot be found in law, for true justice is unchangeable and laws change. It is with laws as with every thing else. If laws are good, why deputies and senators to change them? And if they are bad, why magistrates to apply them?

By the mere fact of being born every human being has a right to live, labor, and be happy. This right of circulating freely in space—the earth under one's feet, the sky above one's head, the sunlight in one's eyes, the air in one's lungs—this primordial right this imprescriptible and natural right anterior to all others, is today denied to millions of human beings.

These millions of disinherited, from whom the rich have taken the earth (the common mother), cannot take a step to the right or left, cannot eat or sleep, cannot, in one word, give free play to their organs, cannot satisfy their needs and live without the permission of other men; their life is always precarious, at the mercy of the caprice of those who have become their masters. They cannot circulate in the great domain of humanity without encountering barriers at every step, without being stopped by these words: "Don't go into that field, it is So-and-so's; don't go into this wood, it belongs to this one; don't pick this fruit, don't catch those fish, they belong to that one."

And if they ask: "Why—then, what have we got?" they will be answered: "Nothing! You have nothing." And already, whilst still quite small, their brains are so fashioned by religion and law that they may accept, without murmuring, this outrageous injustice.

The earth revolves round the sun and presents, alternately, each of its sides to the vivifying influence of that star, but this great revolution is not made for the equal benefit of all human creatures; for the earth belongs to some and not to others, men have bought it with their gold and silver. But by what subterfuge has this been accomplished since gold and silver are contained in the earth with other metals?

How is it that a part can equal in volume the whole?

How is it that, after buying the earth with their gold, they still possess that gold?—*Mystery!!!*

Nor can they have bought, or inherited from their fathers, those immense forests, buried for millions of centuries by geological revolutions; because at that time there was no human being on the earth. Nevertheless it belongs to them; for all, from the depths of the earth and the bottom of the oceans to the highest summits of the great mountains—all belongs to them. Forests formerly grew so that this man might give a dowry to his daughter; geological revolutions took places so that man might give a palace to his mistress; and it was in order that they might drink champagne that those forests were slowly converted to coal.

But if the disinherited should ask: "What shall we do to live if we have a right to nothing?" they are told: "Console yourselves; the possessors are worthy men and, provided you are good, provided you obey all their wishes, they will allow you to live, in return for which you must till their fields, make their clothes, build their houses, shear their sheep, prune their trees, construct machinery, make books—in short, provide all those physical and intellectual pleasures to which they alone have a right. If the rich are kind enough to let you eat their bread and drink their water you must thank them warmly, for you lives belong to them, as well as everything else."

You have no right to live unless it be with their permission, and on condition that you work for them. They will direct you, they will watch you work, they will enjoy the fruits of your toil; for it is their due. All that you may require for your work belongs to them also. While they, born at the same time as you, shall pass their lives commanding, all your lifetime you must obey. Whilst they are able to rest in the shade of trees, poetise on the murmur of rivulets, strengthen their muscles in the water of the sea, seek health at thermal springs, enjoy the splendid views from the height of mountains, enter into possession of the conquests of human intellect and thus converse with those powerful sowers of ideas, those indefatigable seekers of the Beyond, you, when hardly grown our of your first childhood, slaves from birth, you must begin to drag your burden of misery; you must produce, that others may consume; work, that others may be idle; die at your task, that others may live in joy.

Whilst they are able to traverse the earth in all directions, to enjoy all horizons, to live in constant communion with Nature, and to seek at the inexhaustible source of poetry the most refined and sweet sensations that can thrill a human being, you shall have for all your horizon the four walls of your hovels, of your workshops, of the penal settlement or the prison; a mere human machine whose life consists in one act indefinitely repeated, you must recommence each day the task of yesterday, until some wheel breaks in you, or, worn out and old, you are cast into the gutter as unable to provide them with sufficient returns.

Woe to you if illness should cast you down—if, young or old, you should be too weak to produce at the good pleasure of the possessing classes! Woe to you if you should find no one to whom you may prostitute your brain, your arm, your body!— you will fall from abyss to abyss; they will make a crime of your rags, a reproach of your pangs of hunger; the whole of society will hurl anathemas against you, and Authority intervening, law in hand, will cry after you: "Woe to the homeless! Woe to those with no roof to shelter them! Woe to him who has not a bed on which to rest his weary limbs! Woe to him who dares to be hungry when others have overfed! Woe to him who is cold when others are warm! Woe to vagabonds! Woe to the vanquished!" Law will strike them for daring to have nothing while others have all. "It is just," says Law. "It is a crime!" say we: "it must not be, it must cease to exist; for it is unjust."

Too long have men accepted as a moral law the expression of the will of the few and powerful; too long has the wickedness of some found accomplices in the ignorance and cowardice of others; too long have men been deaf to the voice of reason, justice and Nature; too long have they accepted lies as truth. And here is the truth: What is life but a perpetual process of assimilation and dispersion which incorporates with the human being molecules of matter in diverse forms and then soon snatches them away to combine them anew in a thousand different ways; a perpetual process of action and reaction between the individual and his surrounding natural environment, which is composed of all that is not himself: such is life! All things animate and inanimate perpetually tend, by their continuous action, to the absorption of the individual, to the dissolution of his identity, to his death.

Nature only fashions new from old; she always destroys to create; she brings life out of death, and she has to fill what *is* to give birth to what *shall be*. Thus life is only possible for the individual through perpetual reaction between himself and the totality of things which surround him. He can only live on condition of combating the decomposition which all things subject him to, by assimilating to himself new molecules which, in his turn, he must borrow from everything.

And, indeed, all animate objects, at whatever stage of organization they may be, from zoophytes to men, are provided with the requisite faculties for combating the decomposition of their organisms by incorporating in themselves new elements borrowed from the environment in which they live. All are provided with more or less perfect organs designed to prevent the presence of causes likely to bring about too swift a decomposition. All are provided with organs enabling them to fight against the disorganizing influence of the elements.

Why should they be provided with these organs if they are not to use them—if it is not right for them to make use of them?

Let the one side cease to deny the other the right to life and happiness, and prostitution and murder will disappear; for all are born equally free and good. It is the social laws which make men bad and unjust, slaves or masters, robbed and robbers, murderers or victims. Every man is an independent autonomous being, that is why the independence of each should be respected. Every attempt against natural liberty, every enforced restraint, is a crime which calls for revolt.

I am well aware that my argument bears no resemblance to the political economy taught by M. Leroy-Beaulieu, not to the morality of Malthus, nor to the Christian Socialism of [Pope] Leo XIII, who preaches the renunciation of riches while himself surrounded by wealth, and humility while proclaiming himself the first of all men. I am well aware that this natural philosophy runs counter to all generally accepted ideas, be they religious, moral, or political. But its ultimate victory is assured for it is superior to all other philosophical theory, to all other moral conception, *for it vindicates no right for some which it does not equally vindicate for others; and it means true equality, it implies justice.* It does not bend before either time or environment—and does not proclaim the same action both good and bad.

It has nothing in common with that double-faced morality common among men nowadays which decides an action to be good or bad according to the latitude or longitude in which it is performed.

For instance it does not proclaim that it is sometimes atrocious and sometimes sublime to seize a thing and leave behind the corpse of its former owner. Atrocious if it takes place in the neighborhood of Paris, sublime if it takes place in the neighborhood of Havre or Berlin. And as it does not admit of either punishment or reward it does not call for the guillotine on the one hand, or an apotheosis on the other. In place of all the innumerable and ever changing moral laws invented by some to enslave others, and proving their frailty by their very number and instability, it substitutes natural justice, the immutable law of good and evil, which is the work of no man but results from the internal organization of each. The good is that which is good for us, which procures for us pleasurable sensations, and as it is these sensations which determine our will, the good is that which we desire; evil is that which is bad for us, that which gives us painful sensations, it is that which we do not desire. "Do as you wish," is the only law which our justice recognizes; for it proclaims the liberty of each in the equality of all.

Those who think that none would work unless obliged to, forget that inaction is death—that we have energies to expend so as to renew them continuously, and that health and happiness can only be preserved on the condition of activity—that as none wish to be unhappy and ill, all will have to use their organs so as to enjoy all their faculties; for a faculty which is not used does not exist, and that means one source of happiness the less in the life of the individual.

Tomorrow as today, as yesterday, men will wish to be happy, they will always expend their energy, they will always work; but as the work of all will be productive of social wealth, the happiness of all and each will be augmented thereby and thus each will be able to enjoy the luxury he has a right to; for there is no such thing as the superfluous, and all that can exist is necessary.

Man is not only a stomach, he has also a brain; he requires books, pictures, statues, music, poetry, just as he requires bread, air and sunlight; but, just as in his consumption he must only be limited by his power of consumption, so, in his production, he must only be limited by his power of production, and as he consumes according to his needs he must produce according to his capacity. Now who can know his needs better than himself? Who can know his capacity better than himself? No one: consequently man must produce and consume according to his own will.

Humanity has always had the latent knowledge that it could only be happy and that all the beautiful qualities of human nature would only be able to expand under Communism.

Thus the golden age of the ancients was based on common property, and it never occurred to the choicest natures who have poetized the past that the happiness of man was compatible with private property. They knew by intuition or experience that all the evils and vices of humanity arise from the antagonism of interests created by individual appropriation unlimited by needs, and they never dreamt of a society without wars, without murders, without prostitution, without crime and without vice, which was not also without property owners.

It is because we wish for no more wars, no murders, no prostitution, no vice, no crime, that we struggle for human liberty and dignity. In spite of all gags the word of truth will ring through the world, and men will thrill at its sound, they will rise at the call of Liberty to be the artisans of their own happiness. So, indeed, we are strong in our very weakness; for, whatever may happen, we shall conquer.

Our enslavement teaches men that they have a right to revolt; our imprisonment, that they have a right to freedom; and by our death they learn that they have a right to live.

Presently, when we shall return to prison and you will return to your families, superficial observers will think that we are the conquered. An error: we are the men of the future, and you are the men of the past.

We represent tomorrow, and you yesterday; and no one has the power to prevent each minute that goes by from bringing nearer the morrow and distancing yesterday. Yesterday has always tried to bar the way of the morrow and it has always been conquered in its very victory; for the time it had passed in conquering has brought it nearer to its defeat.

*It* made Socrates drink the hemlock; *it* made Galileo recant under pain of torture; *it* burnt John Huss, Stephen Dolct, William of Prague, Giordano Bruno; *it* guillotined [Jacques] Hébert, [François-Noël] Babeuf; *it* poisoned [Louis] Blanqui; *it* shot [Gustave] Flourens and [Théophile] Ferré. What were the names of the judges of Socrates, of Galileo, of John Huss, of William of Prague, of Stephen Dolct, of Giordano Bruno, of

Hébert, of Babeuf, of Blanqui, of Flourens, of Ferré? No one knows: they are the past; they were already dead whilst they yet lived. They have not even attained the fame of Erostrates; whilst Socrates is immortal, whilst Galileo yet lives, whilst John Huss exists, whilst William of Prague, Giordano Bruno, Stephen Dolct, Hébert, Babeuf, Blanqui, Flourens, and Ferré live.

Thus we shall be in our misfortune, triumphant in our misery, victorious in our defeat. We shall be happy, no matter what happens; for we are certain that at the breath of the renovating idea others will be brought to the truth, other men will undertake our interrupted task and bring it to a good end; and, finally, that a day will come when the star which gilds the harvests will shine on Humanity without armies, without cannons, without frontiers, without barriers, without prisons, without magistrates, without police, without laws and without gods; free at last intellectually and physically, and men, reconciled with Nature and themselves, will at last be able to quench their thirst for justice in the universal harmony.

What matters it if the dawn of this great day be impurpled by the glow of fires; what matters it that in the morning of that day the dew be bloody? The tempest also is useful to purify the atmosphere; the sun shines more brightly after the storm.

And the glorious sun of Liberty will shine and Humanity will be happy. Then, each sheltering his individual happiness behind the universal happiness, no one will do evil; for it will be to no one's advantage to do evil.

Free man amidst enfranchised Humanity will be able to march unhindered from victory to victory for the good of all towards the unbounded infinity of his intellectual powers.

The riddle of today—Liberty, Equality, Fraternity—set by the Sphinx of the [French] Revolution, when solved will be—*Anarchy!*

Auguste Vaillant

DEPOT DES C

## AUGUSTE VAILLANT 1894

AUGUSTE VAILLANT WAS A FRENCH ANARCHIST, who took revenge for the execution of Ravachol by throwing a homemade bomb into the Chamber of Deputies in Paris. The bomb didn't kill anyone, but merely injured twenty Deputies, along with injuring Vaillant himself. Vaillant never denied throwing the bomb, taking credit for the act, and explaining his reasoning to the court. Vaillante was the first execution in decades that France carried out for a crime that didn't result in death.

---

Gentlemen, in a few minutes you are to deal your blow, but in receiving your verdict I shall at least have the satisfaction of having injured the existing society, this cursed society in which one may see a single man uselessly spending enough to feed thousands of families; an infamous society that permits a few individuals to monopolize all social wealth, while there are hundreds of thousands of unfortunates who have not even the bread that is not refused to dogs, and while entire families are committing suicide for want of the necessities of life.

Ah, gentlemen, if the governing classes could go down among the unfortunates! But no, they prefer to remain deaf to their appeals. It seems that a fatality impels them, like the royalty of the eighteenth century, toward the precipice that will engulf them, for woe on those who remain deaf to the cries of the starving, woe on those who, believing themselves of superior essence, assume the right to exploit those beneath them! There comes a time when the people no longer reason; they rise like a hurricane, and pass away like a torrent. Then we see bleeding heads impaled on pikes.

Among the exploited, gentlemen, there are two classes of individuals. Those of one class, not realizing what they are and what they might be, take life as it comes, believe that they are born to be slaves, and content themselves with the little that is given them in exchange for their labor. But there are others, on the contrary, who think, who study, and who, looking about them, discover social iniquities. Is it their fault if they see clearly and suffer at seeing others suffer? Then they throw themselves into the struggle, and make themselves the bearers of the popular claims. Gentlemen, I am one of the latter. Wherever I have gone, I have seen unfortunates bent beneath the yoke of capital. Everywhere I have seen the same wounds causing tears of blood to flow, even in the remoter parts of the inhabited districts of South America, where I had the right to believe that he who was weary of the pains of civilization might rest in the shade of the palm trees and there study nature. Well, there even, more than elsewhere, I have seen capital come, like a vampire, to suck the last drop of blood of the unfortunate pariahs.

Then I came back to France, where I was forced to see my family suffer atrociously. This was the last drop in the cup of my sorrow. Tired of leading this life of suffering and cowardice, I carried this bomb to those who are primarily responsible for social misery.

I am reproached with the wounds of those who were struck by my projectiles. Permit me to point out in passing that, if the bourgeois had not massacred or caused massacres during the Revolution, it is probable that they would still be under the yoke of the nobility. On the other hand, figure up the dead and wounded in Tonkin, Madagascar, Dahomey, adding to this the thousands, yes, millions of unfortunates who die in the factories, the mines, and wherever the grinding power of capital is felt. Add also those who die of hunger, and all this with the assent of our Deputies. Beside all this, of how little weight are the reproaches now brought against me!

It is true that one does not efface the other; but, after all, are we not acting on the defensive when we respond to the blows that we receive from above? I know very well that I shall be told that I ought to have confined myself to speech for the vindication of the people's claims. But what can you expect! It takes a loud voice to make the deaf hear. Too long have they answered our voices by imprisonment, the rope, and rifle volleys. Make no mistake; the explosion of my bomb is not only the cry of the rebel Vaillant, but the cry of an entire class that vindicates its rights, and that will soon add acts to words. For, be sure of it, in vain will they pass laws. The ideas of the thinkers will not halt. Just as, in the last century, all the governmental forces could not prevent the Diderots and the Voltaires from spreading emancipating ideas among the people, so all the existing governmental forces will not prevent the Reclus, the Darwins, the Spencers, the Ibsens, the Mirbeaus from spreading the ideas of justice and liberty that will annihilate the prejudices that hold the mass in ignorance. And these ideas, welcomed by the unfortunate, will flower in acts of revolt as they have done in me, until the day when the disappearance of authority shall permit all men to organize freely according to their choice, when everyone shall be able to enjoy the product of his labor, and when those moral maladies called prejudices shall vanish, permitting human beings to live in harmony, having no other desire than to study the sciences and love their fellows.

I conclude, gentlemen, by saying that a society in which one sees such social inequalities as we see all about us, in which we every day see suicides caused by poverty, prostitution flaring at every street corner, a society whose principal monuments are barracks and prisons: such a society must be transformed as soon as possible, on pain of being eliminated, and that speedily, from the human race. Hail to him who labors, by no matter what means, for this transformation! It is this idea that has guided me in my duel with authority, but as in this duel I have only wounded my adversary, it is now its turn to strike me.

Now, gentlemen, to me it matters little what penalty you may inflict, for, looking at this assembly with the eyes of reason, I cannot help smiling to see you, atoms lost in matter, and reasoning only because you possess a prolongation of the spinal marrow, assume the right to judge one of your fellows.

Ah! gentlemen, how small a thing is your assembly and your verdict in the history of humanity; and human history, in its turn, is likewise a very little thing in the whirlwind that bears it through immensity, and that is destined to disappear, or at least to be transformed, in order to begin again the same history and the same facts, a veritably perpetual play of cosmic forces renewing and transferring themselves forever.

When Vaillant was awakened to be led to his death, he told the authorities that his "body is nothing, I shall be revenged." He was right. Before being placed in to the guillotine, Vaillant yelled out *"Death to the Bourgeoisie, Long Live Anarchy!"*

**ÉMILE HENRY 1894**

ÉMILE HENRY WAS BORN IN BARCELONA TO A father that fled France because of repression against those who supported the Paris Commune. Raised the son (and brother) of radicals, Henry joined the anarchist movement in France at a young age. In 1892, he attempted to bomb the offices of a mining company that was the target of a labor strike, but police found the bomb first, resulting in the death of five officers. In 1894, following the execution of Auguste Vaillant, and a massive amount of state repression against anarchists that followed, Henry decided to bomb the Café Terminus, a popular bourgeois hangout, during a concert. The explosion killed one person and injured twenty.

---

It is not a defense that I present to you. I am not in any way seeking to escape the reprisals of the society I have attacked. Besides, I acknowledge only one tribunal—myself—and the verdict of any other is meaningless to me. I wish merely to give you an explanation of my acts and to tell you how I was led to perform them.

I have been an anarchist for only a short time. It was as recently as the middle of 1891 that I entered the revolutionary movement. Up to that time, I had lived in circles entirely imbued with current morality. I had been accustomed to respect and even to love the principles of fatherland and family, of authority and property.

For teachers in the present generation too often forget one thing: it is that life, with its struggles and defeats, its injustices and iniquities, takes upon itself indiscreetly to open the eyes of the ignorant to reality. This happened to me, as it happens to everyone. I had been told that life was easy, that it was wide open to those who were intelligent and energetic; experience showed me that only the cynical and the servile were able to secure good seats at the banquet.

I had been told that our social institutions were founded on justice and equality; I observed all around me nothing but lies and impostures.

Each day I shed an illusion. Everywhere I went, I witnessed the same miseries among some, and the same joys among others. I was not slow to understand that the grand words I had been taught to venerate: honor, devotion, duty, were only the mask that concealed the most shameful baseness.

The manufacturer who created a colossal fortune out of the toil of workers who lacked everything was an honest gentleman. The deputy and the minister, their hands ever open for bribes, were devoted to the public good. The officer who experimented with a new type of rifle on children of seven had done his duty, and, openly in parliament, the president of the council congratulated him! Everything I saw revolted me, and my intelligence was attracted by criticism of the existing social organization. Such criticism has been made too often for me to repeat it. It is enough to say that I became the enemy of a society that I judged to be criminal.

Drawn at first to socialism, I was not slow in separating

myself from that party. I have too much love of freedom, too much respect for individual initiative, too much repugnance for military organization to assume a number in the ordered army of the fourth estate. Besides, I realized that basically socialism changes nothing in the existing order. It maintains the principle of authority, and, whatever self-styled free-thinkers may say about it, that principle is no more than the antiquated survival of faith in a superior power.

Scientific studies gradually made me aware of the play of natural forces in the universe. I became materialist and atheist; I came to realize that modern science discards the hypothesis of God, of which it has no need. In the same way, religious and authoritarian morality, which are based on false assumptions, should be allowed to disappear. What then, I asked myself, was the new morality in harmony with the laws of nature that might regenerate the old world and give birth to a happy humanity?

It was at this moment that I came into contact with a group of anarchist comrades whom I consider, even today, among the best I have ever known. The character of these men immediately captivated me. I discerned in them a great sincerity, a total frankness, a searching distrust of all prejudices, and I wanted to understand the idea that produced men so different from anyone I had encountered up to that point.

The idea—as soon as I embraced it—found in my mind a soil completely prepared by observation and personal reflection to receive it. It merely gave precision to what already existed there in vague and wavering form. In my turn I became an anarchist.

I do not need to develop on this occasion the whole theory of anarchism. I merely wish to emphasize its revolutionary aspect, the destructive and negative aspect that brings me here before you.

At this moment of embittered struggle between the middle class and its enemies, I am almost tempted to say, with Souvarine in *Germinal*: "All discussions about the future are criminal, since they hinder pure and simple destruction and slow down the march of the revolution."

I brought with me into the struggle a profound hatred, which every day was renewed by the spectacle of this society where everything is base, everything is equivocal, everything is ugly, where everything is an impediment to the outflow of human passions, to the generous impulses of the heart, to the free flight of thought.

I wanted to strike as strongly and as justly as I could. Let us start then with the first attempt I made, the explosion in the Rue des Bon-Enfants. I had followed closely the events at Carmaux. The first news of the strike had filled me with joy. The miners seemed at last to have abandoned those useless pacifist strikes in which the trusting worker patiently waits for his few francs to triumph over the company's millions. They seemed to have gone down the path of violence that manifested itself resolutely on August 15, 1892. The offices and buildings of the mine were invaded by a crowd of people tired of suffering without reprisals; justice was about to be wrought on the engineer whom his workers so deeply hated, when the timorous ones chose to interfere.

Who were these men? The same who cause the miscarriage of all revolutionary movements because they fear that the people, once they act freely, will no longer obey their voices; those who persuade thousands of men to endure privations month after month so as to beat the drum over their sufferings and create for themselves a popularity that will put them into office: such men—I mean the socialist leaders—in fact assumed the leadership of the strike movement.

Immediately a wave of glib gentlemen appeared in the region; they put themselves entirely at the disposition of the struggle, organized subscriptions, arranged conferences, and appealed on all sides for funds. The miners surrendered all initiative into their hands, and what happened, everyone knows.

The strike went on and on, and the miners established the

most intimate acquaintance with hunger, which became their habitual companion; they used up the tiny reserve fund of their syndicate and of the other organizations that came to their help, and then, at the end of two months, they returned crestfallen to their pit, more wretched than ever before. It would have been so simple in the beginning to have attacked the Company in its only sensitive spot, the financial one; to have burnt the stocks of coal, to have broken the mining machines, to have demolished the drainage pumps.

Then, certainly, the Company would have very soon capitulated. But the great pontiffs of socialism would not allow such procedures because they are anarchist procedures. At such games one runs the risk of prison and—who knows?—perhaps one of those bullets that performed so miraculously at Fourmies? That is not the way to win seats on municipal councils or in legislatures. In brief, having been momentarily troubled, order reigned once again at Carmaux.

More powerful than ever, the Company continued its exploitation, and the gentlemen shareholders congratulated themselves on the happy outcome of the strike. Their dividends would be even more pleasant to gather in.

It was then that I decided to intrude among that concert of happy tones a voice the bourgeois had already heard but which they thought had died with Ravachol: the voice of dynamite.

I wanted to show the bourgeoisie that henceforward their pleasures would not be untouched, that their insolent triumphs would be disturbed, that their golden calf would rock violently on its pedestal until the final shock that would cast it down among filth and blood.

At the same time I wanted to make the miners understand that there is only one category of men, the anarchists, who sincerely resent their sufferings and are willing to avenge them. Such men do not sit in parliament like Monsieur Guesde and his associates, but they march to the guillotine.

So I prepared a bomb. At one stage the accusation that had been thrown at Ravachol came to my memory. What about the innocent victims? I soon resolved that question. The building where the Carmaux Company had its offices was inhabited only by bourgeois; hence there would be no innocent victims. The whole of the bourgeoisie lives by the exploitation of the unfortunate, and should expiate its crimes together. So it was with absolute confidence in the legitimacy of my deed that I left my bomb before the door to the Company's offices.

I have already explained my hope, in case my device was discovered before it exploded, that it would go off in the police station, where those it harmed would still be my enemies. Such were the motives that led me to commit the first attempt of which I have been accused.

Let us go on to the second incident, of the Café Terminus. I had returned to Paris at the time of the Vaillant affair, and I witnessed the frightful repression that followed the explosion at the Palais Bourbon. I saw the draconian measures that the government decided to take against the anarchists. Everywhere there were spies, and searches, and arrests. A crowd of individuals were indiscriminately rounded up, torn from their families, and thrown into prison. Nobody was concerned about what happened to the wives and children of these comrades while they remained in jail.

The anarchist was no longer regarded as a man, but as a wild beast to be hunted everywhere while the bourgeois press, which is the vile slave of authority, loudly demands his extermination.

At the same time, anarchist papers and pamphlets were seized and the right of meeting was abrogated. Worse than that: when it seemed desirable to get one comrade completely out of the way, an informer came and left in his room a packet that he said contained tannin; the next day a search was made, on a warrant dated the previous day, a box of suspicious powders was found, the comrade was taken to court and sentenced to three years in jail. If you wish to know the truth of that, ask the wretched spy who found his way into the home of comrade Mérigeaud!

But all such procedures were good because they struck at an enemy who had spread fear, and those who had trembled wanted to display their courage. As the crown of that crusade against the heretics, we heard M. Reynal, Minister of the Interior, declare in the Chamber of Deputies that the measures taken by the government had thrown terror into the camp of the anarchists. But that was not yet enough.

A man who had killed nobody was condemned to death. It was necessary to appear brave right to the end, and one fine morning he was guillotined.

But, gentlemen of the bourgeoisie, you have reckoned a little too much without your host. You arrested hundreds of men and women, you violated scores of homes, but still outside the prison walls there were men unknown to you who watched from the shadows as you hunted the anarchists, and waited only for the moment that would be favorable for them in their turn to hunt the hunters.

Reynal's words were a challenge thrown before the anarchists. The gauntlet was taken up. The bomb in the Café Terminus is the answer to all your violations of freedom, to your arrests, to your searches, to your laws against the press, to your mass transportations, to your guillotinings. But why, you ask, attack these peaceful café guests, who sat listening to music and who, no doubt, were neither judges nor deputies nor bureaucrats? Why? It is very simple. The bourgeoisie did not distinguish among the anarchists. Vaillant, a man on his own, threw a bomb; nine tenths of the comrades did not even know him. But that meant nothing; the persecution was a mass one, and anyone with the slightest anarchist links was hunted down. And since you hold a whole party responsible for the actions of a single man, and strike indiscriminately, we also strike indiscriminately.

Perhaps we should attack only the deputies who make laws against us, the judges who apply those laws, the police who arrest us? I do not agree. These men are only instruments. They do not act in their own name. Their functions were instituted by the bourgeoisie for its own defense. They are no more guilty than the rest of you. Those good bourgeois who hold no office but who reap their dividends and live idly on the profits of the workers' toil, they also must take their share in the reprisals. And not only they, but all those who are satisfied with the existing order, who applaud the acts of the government and so become its accomplices, those clerks earning three or five hundred francs a month who hate the people even more violently than the rich, that stupid and pretentious mass of folk who always choose the strongest side—in other words, the daily clientele of Terminus and the other great cafés.

That is why I struck at random and did not choose my victims! The bourgeoisie must be brought to understand that those who have suffered have finally grown tired of their sufferings; they are showing their teeth and they will strike all the more brutally if you are brutal with them. They have no respect for human life, because the bourgeoisie themselves have shown they have no care for it. It is not for the assassins who were responsible for the bloody week and for Fourmies to regard others as assassins.

We will not spare the women and children of the bourgeois, for the women and children of those we love have not been spared. Must we not count among the innocent victims those children who die slowly of anemia in the slums because bread is scarce in their houses; those women who grow pale in your workshops, working to earn forty *sous* a day and fortunate when poverty does not force them into prostitution; those old men whom you have made production machines all their lives and whom you cast onto the waste heap or into the workhouse when their strength has worn away?

At least have the courage of your crimes, gentlemen of the bourgeoisie, and grant that our reprisals are completely legitimate.

Of course, I am under no illusions. I know my deeds will not yet be understood by the masses who are unprepared for them. Even among the workers, for whom I have fought, there will be many, misled by your newspapers, who will regard me as their enemy. But that does not matter. I am not concerned with anyone's judgment. Nor am I ignorant of the fact that there are individuals claiming to be anarchists who hasten to disclaim any solidarity with the propagandists of the deed. They seek to establish a subtle distinction between the theoreticians and the terrorists. Too cowardly to risk their own lives, they deny those who act. But the influence they pretend to wield over the revolutionary movement is nil. Today the field is open to action, without weakness or retreat.

Alexander Herzen, the Russian revolutionary, once said: "Of two things one must be chosen: to condemn and march forward, or to pardon and turn back halfway." We intend neither to pardon nor to turn back, and we shall always march forward until the revolution, which is the goal of our efforts, finally arrives to crown our work with the creation of a free world.

In that pitiless war that we have declared on the bourgeoisie, we ask for no pity. We give death, and we know how to endure it. So it is with indifference that I await your verdict. I know that my head is not the last you will cut off; yet others will fall, for the starving are beginning to know the way to your great cafés and restaurants, to the Terminus and Foyot. You will add other names to the bloody list of our dead.

You have hanged in Chicago, decapitated in Germany, garroted in Jerez, shot in Barcelona, guillotined in Montbrison and Paris, but what you will never destroy is anarchy. Its roots are too deep. It is born in the heart of a society that is rotting and falling apart. It is a violent reaction against the established order. It represents all the egalitarian and libertarian aspirations that strike out against authority. It is everywhere, which makes it impossible to contain. It will end by killing you.

On the way to guillotine, Henry cried out "*Courage comrades! Vive l'anarchie!*"

## SANTE CASERIO 1894

SANTE CASERIO WAS AN ITALIAN-BORN ANARchist who left home at the age of 10 to become an anarchist baker. After an eight month jail sentence for distributing anarchist propaganda, Caserio fled Italy, eventually making his way to France. In 1894, Caserio plunged a red and black knife into the president of France, in retaliation for repression and execution of anarchists. While being interrogated, the police asked Caserio to give dirt on other anarchists, but Caserio said that he was "a baker, never an informer." He was found guilty of regicide, and executed by guillotine on August 16, 1894, at the age of 20.

---

Gentlemen of the jury, I'm not going to defend myself but rather explain my action.

While still young I learned that today's society is poorly organized, so poorly that every day many unfortunates commit suicide, leaving wives and children in the most terrible distress. Workers in their thousands look for work and can't find any. Poor families beg for their food and shiver from the cold. They suffer the worst poverty. The youngest ask their poor mothers for food and the latter can't give them any because they don't have anything. The few things that were in the house were already sold or traded. All they can do is ask for alms; they're often arrested for vagabondage.

I left my native land because I was often brought to tears upon seeing little girls of eight or ten forced to work fifteen hours a day for a miserable wage of twenty centimes. Young women of eighteen or twenty also work twenty hours a day for a laughable salary. And this doesn't only happen to my compatriots, but to all workers who sweat all day long for a morsel of bread while their labor brings in money in abundance. The workers are forced to live under the most wretched conditions and their food consists of a bit of bread, a few spoonfuls of rice, and water. And so when they reach the age of thirty or forty they're dying of fatigue and die in hospitals. What's more, as a consequence of their poor diets and overwork these sad creature are devoured in their hundreds by pellagra, an illness that, in my country, attacks, as the doctors say, those who are malnourished and who lead a hard and deprived existence.

I saw that there are some people who are hungry and some children who suffer while food and clothing are abundant in the cities. I saw several great industries full of clothing and wool products and I also saw warehouses full of wheat and corn that would be suitable for those who needed them. And from another point of view, I saw thousands of people who don't work, who produce nothing, and who live thanks to the labor of others; who every day spend thousands of francs to amuse themselves; who corrupt the daughters of workers; who own lodgings with forty or fifty rooms, twenty or thirty horses, and several servants: in a word, all the pleasures of life.

I believe in God, but when I see such inequality among men I recognize that it isn't God who created man but man who created God. And I discovered that those who want their property respected have an interest in preaching paradise and hell and keeping the people in a state of ignorance.

A short time ago, Vaillant threw a bomb in the Chamber of Deputies in protest against the current system of society. He killed no one and only wounded a few people. But bourgeois justice condemned him to death. And not satisfied with the condemnation of the guilty man, it pursued the anarchists and arrested not only those who knew Vaillant but even those who attended an anarchist lecture.

The government didn't think of their wives and children. It didn't consider that a man held in a cell isn't the only one to suffer, that his little ones ask for bread. Bourgeois justice didn't trouble itself with these innocents, who don't even know what society is. It's not their fault if their fathers are in prison; all they want to do is eat.

The government went so far as to search people's private homes, to open personal letters, to prohibit lectures and meetings, and practiced the most infamous oppression against us. Even today hundreds of anarchists are arrested for having written a newspaper article or for having expressed an opinion in public.

Well then, if the government employs guns, chains, and prisons against us, must we anarchists, who defend our lives, remain locked in our houses? No. On the contrary, we answer governments with dynamite, bombs, the stylus, and the dagger. In a word, we must do all we can to destroy the bourgeoisie and government. Gentlemen of the jury, you who are the representatives of bourgeois society, if you want my head, take it. But don't think that in doing so you are stopping the anarchist movement.

Beware: man reaps what he sows.

On the way to guillotine, Caserio declared "*Courage cousins! Vive l'anarchie!*"

-217. 662

Félix Fénéon

**FÉLIX FÉNÉON 1894**

IN THE MIDST OF THE RASH OF BOMBINGS COM-mitted by anarchists in Paris in the years after the Clichy Affair, in addition to the assassination of the president by the Italian anarchist Sante Caserio, the French government launched a rash of repression. Large numbers of anarchists were rounded up with no pretext other than that they were anarchists. Félix Fénéon was a writer, publisher, art critic, and a clerk at the Ministry of War, who was caught up in the repression. He briefly worked on the indi-vidualist paper *l'Endehors* after it's founder Zo d'Axa fled the repression in France. Fénéon was tried with twenty-nine others in what became known as the Trial of the Thirty. This farce of a trial wound up resulting in the acquittal of twenty-seven of the defendants, including Fénéon.

---

**COURT:** *Are you an anarchist, Monsieur Fénéon?*

**FF:** I am a Burgundian, born in Turin.

**COURT:** *By a very astonishing contrast, you, the model clerk of*

*the Ministry of War, you were one of the active collaborators of*
l'Endehors?

**FF:** This is absolutely inaccurate. I have only written, from time
to time, some fine art articles and a humorous study of le Chat
Noir. [Laughter]

The editor-in-chief of *l'Endehors*, Mr. Zo d'Axa, was my
personal friend. My collaboration goes back to a period long
ago, when the newspaper had not yet taken a distinct character.

**COURT:** *You could not be unaware, however, that this paper was
intended to insult the army. And you did not hesitate to contribute, you, an employee of the Ministry of War!*

*You were Zo d'Axa's friend, you say, you were also the close
friend of the anarchist [Alexander] Cohen, who expressed
regret at the arrival of the Russians and the funeral of Marshall
MacMahon that "...all this chauvinism" was not put to the boil
by the "crowd"?*

*You know that letter, do you not?*

**FF:** I do not have the quality to discuss Mr. Cohen's epistolary
fantasies. Also, the letter you speak of was not addressed to me!

**COURT:** *Never mind. These are, I repeat, odd relations for an
employee in the Ministry of War.*

*You were also the friend of an anarchist named Kampfmeyer,
the leader of the "youth party" in Berlin.*

**FF:** Kampfmeyer does not know French; I do not know German.
Our conversations could not be very subversive. [*Laughter*]

**COURT:** *You also knew and visited [Louis] Matha, the former ed-
itorial director of* l'Endehors, *a refugee in London following a sentence to two years in prison for inciting soldiers to insubordination.*

*You saw him last January, when he returned to France a few days before the Café Terminus explosion. By the way, Matha must have been charged with a very important mission to risk his liberty!*

*It's at your house that Matha showed up at the beginning of this secretive journey, and you gave him the key to Cohen's former home, where he kept himself hidden for several weeks.*

**FF:** This key did not belong to me. Cohen had entrusted it to me, imploring me to give it to Matha. Simple, as you see.

I add that Matha was not hiding much. He could be encountered at 10:00 in the morning on the streets, with his exuberant beard and extraordinary overcoat, alone enough to pick him out.

**COURT:** *Why, if things are so ordinary, did you initially pretend that you did not know him?*

**FF:** The day I was arrested, I systematically answered "no" to all the questions I was asked. It would have been at least decent to give me time to recover and get used to handcuffs. [*Laughter*] I am reluctant to give information about anyone. If you had asked me about Mr. Chairman, I would have observed the same reservation.

**COURT:** *And Ortiz? He was your friend as well?*

**FF:** You use words far too strong. Ortiz has never been my friend. I met him two or three times in a group of young people where literature and weapons were being made. I did not even remember his face when he was brought here.

**COURT:** *It has been established that you surrounded yourself with Cohen and Ortiz.*

**FF:** One can hardly be surrounded by two persons; you need at least three. [*More laughter*]

**COURT:** *You were seen conferring with them behind a lamppost!*

**FF:** A lamppost is round. Can Your Honour tell me where *behind* a lamppost is?" [*Loud, prolonged laughter, Judge calls for order*]

**COURT:** *Your informer, however, asserts that Ortiz came to your house often, and that you receive, besides, a crowd of suspicious people.*

**FF:** These suspicious people were painters and poets. The informer may not have enough quality to judge them.

**COURT:** *Finally, you knew Émile Henry. Did you not tell Cohen that you met him?*

**FF:** I never saw Émile Henry at Cohen's.

**COURT:** *Here is the anarchist milieu that you surrounded yourself with after leaving the Ministry of War!*
   *As a result of what circumstances did you find yourself there?*

**FF:** Through a legitimate curiosity in Symbolism [19th century art movement] and Impressionism. Moreover, in the midst of *l'Endehors*, there were infinitely fewer anarchists than writers and painters.

**COURT:** *You know that eleven detonators and a bottle of mercury have been found in your office at the Ministry of War.*
   *How did you find yourself in possession of such substances?*

**FF:** I found this bottle of mercury and tin tubes in March 1894, by clearing the bedroom of my father who had just died.

**COURT:** *Did you not also take three boxes full of letters to the Ministry of War?*

**FF:** That's right, but not one of these letters came from a recognized anarchist.

**COURT:** *And why did you not leave all that at home?*

**FF:** I was dreading a search because of my relationship with Cohen, and I did not want to stay in jail for two months, waiting for the prosecution to find all this correspondence.

The mercury tube and the detonators were, by chance, bundled with it. There was also a medal of St. Helena and the skin of a black cat. [*prolonged laughter*] I repeat to you that I found all this in the affairs of my father, which I had not yet had the leisure to sort.

**COURT:** *Your mother and maid claimed that your father found these tin tubes in the street. It is very surprising that we can find machines filled with dynamite in the street?*

**FF:** You think? Well! Judge Meyer asked me why I hadn't thrown them out the window instead of taking them to the Ministry. So you see, it is possible to find detonators in the street. [*Laughter*]

Besides, these tubes were enclosed in a kind of matchbox, which was in my father's room, in the midst of his jokes and his pipes. I never opened this box.

**COURT:** *Your father, an employee of the Banque de France, would never have kept explosive devices at home!*

**FF:** No more than his son, an employee of the Ministry of War.

**COURT:** *Mr. Advocate General will tell you that this is not true, that you hold these devices for an individual who has entrusted them to you, and whom you do not want to name.*

**FF:** I strictly maintain my version of the story.

The court is passing the bottle of mercury around, a small blue bottle, whose label has been torn, and the eleven tin tubes, which look like very thin mechanical pencils.

**COURT:** *[Showing the bottle] Did this little bottle not belong to Émile Henry?*
*You know that it was presented to him and that he admitted having identical bottles in his possession; same color of glass, same type of bottle.*

**FF:** You could have shown him a *muid* [archaic French measurment, about 280 liters] of mercury, and he would have said that it was his as well. It was well within his trickster personality.

**COURT:** *Mr. Girard is convinced that this is one of the bottles that were removed from the villa Faucheur, after the explosion of the Café Terminus, by unknown accomplices of Émile Henry.*
*Did you suppose that the law would not go looking for these bottles at the Ministry of War?*

**FF:** The evidence is that there was a search!
*[With a bored look]* I already told you that I kept all of these items like trinkets!

**COURT:** *According to the experts each of these eleven detonators* *constitutes a dangerous device. Mr. Girard said one of these tubes would blow a box to bits.*

**FF:** I know it now. I did not know it then.

**COURT:** *Mercury is used to make explosives?*

**FF:** And barometers. [*Laughter*] I certainly would not have kept all these things if I had been informed about their nature!

Malatesta awaits trial
in London, 1912

**ERRICO MALATESTA 1898 & 1921**

Errico Malatesta was an Italian anarchist, born in 1853. He spent his entire life agitating for anarchist revolution, spending much of his time in court or in prison for his efforts.

In January of 1898, bread riots occurred in ~50 Italian towns, and spread to the town of Ancona, where Malatesta was residing and publishing the paper *L'Agitazione* with other comrades. On the second day of the riots, Malatesta and three others were arrested and charged with being a criminal association, on the pretext that they encouraged the rioting.

---

My cause is that of my co-accused. I come with my poor and unadorned words to break the spell woven by the splendid pleadings of so many masters of jurisprudence and eloquence. But I speak all the same and without fear, because I have confidence in your fairness and because, besides the arguments of the legal documents submitted to you by my counsels, I want to add to the evidence that must contribute to shape your conviction the document I am offering you—the document of my thoughts. I mean that this may inform a fair judgment of the moral standard of those whom you are asked to shame with the convict's uniform. It strikes me as only fair that you should hear something of our ideas from the most authentic source. I will not conceal the very serious quandary in which I find myself. You have seen that the charge has not even the shadow of a shadow to support it. I am demanding the protection of the law, I seek justice from people whose functions I do not acknowledge, since I do not acknowledge the law, believing, as Dalas has it, that a law works effectively only when it is sanctioned by custom, which is to say, when it is useless. But once a custom has no longer reason to exist in the moral and material conditions of the population, the law becomes an instrument of tyranny. I would like to see your role as judges abolished, because I believe that in a better organized society the role you are now fulfilling will be made redundant, since there will be no more crimes deriving from the populations' economic imbalance, while the remaining ones will be entrusted to the care of psychiatric science.

But as long as the law exists, it must be equal for all; as long as there are courts they must rise above base political passions lest they become police instruments. At any rate, you, Mr. Presiding Judge, need to form an idea of what I am. I have the utmost confidence in you, which derives from the even-handed and truly admirable manner in which you have conducted these proceedings; and you will allow me to thank you, together with this array of valiant counsels who have rallied to defend us and, more than just us, freedom itself.

Let me thank also the honorable public prosecutor, with no hint of irony, because he, a little grudgingly, had nevertheless to concede that we are honest. Out of regard for our honesty, in order to reconcile his belief in our honesty with his official duties, as he conceives them, he had to enunciate the brand new theory according to which criminals are not malefactors.

These men are criminals and I am supposed to be their leader and an evil man; are my hands dripping blood, though? Are my hands stained with thievery? Have I ever sinned against property? When the public prosecutor arrived in this courtroom, he must have been thinking that he would face brigands and must then have been surprised, when he came face to face with a very modest thinker, but an honest and sincere thinker for all that. Whereupon the public prosecutor lost his temper and uttered the ill-advised words: we need to look into Errico Malatesta's thought; an ill-advised thing to say these days, while a square of Rome is overlooked by the statue of Giordano Bruno, a man convicted for a crime of thought.

If we lived in the year 1600, the public prosecutor, too, would pronounce here his *Punietur* and Clement would have erected another stake, just as the Clement of today called for the mild punishment of three years' imprisonment.[1]

But from what sources has the public prosecutor deduced my thought? Has he produced documentation? Far be it from me to give a procedural lesson to such an eminent counsel for the prosecution; I have little and sparse knowledge of procedure, learned during my frequent visits to Italian prisons and courtrooms.

But I mean to put a query to the public prosecutor: he has produced documents, as if they were by Errico Malatesta, and he has built his entire indictment upon what was said in those documents. Does he not think that it would have been proper to check first if they were actually written by me; should he not have had the investigating magistrate show them to me, so that I could either recognize them or repudiate them and prove that they were not mine? That would have behooved him even if those documents had borne my name, since a printed name does not constitute legal evidence; it behooved him even more to ask me, since the texts are anonymous. Even during the public hearings, the

---

1  In the year 1600, Pope Clement VIII gave his consent to the conviction for heresy of the philosopher Giordano Bruno, who was burned alive. The Latin word *punietur* means "let him be punished."

public prosecutor neglected to ask if the texts he was using were mine or not. If criminal proceedings are conducted so lightly, it is to be expected that mistakes be made, and the public prosecutor will now regret having made such a blunder. He even produced a newspaper from Paterson—which is in North America, in the New York area—that contains a piece with which I acquainted myself only yesterday, when it was read out here. It is an anarchist newspaper and its ideas may be shared by some anarchists; am I to be answerable, though, for everything written by anarchists in every corner of the globe? In that case, I myself could supply you with enough evidence to send me to a penal colony for life; because some anarchists have written all sorts of things, and because some anarchists—who, as workers, are part of the most suffering and ignorant population—cannot clearly express their thought and may well think differently from me.

The public prosecutor has a very wrong idea of what the anarchist party is. The proof that he does not know what anarchy means is that he referred to me as a "leader," whereas, if I set myself up as a leader, all these comrades would turn on me!

The public prosecutor was so convinced that among the anarchists there were leaders (it had not even occurred to him to make the slightest effort to check: if such an association existed, I would be the leader) that he imagined I was also the leader of the anarchists of North America and that everything that is written about anarchy is written at my command. Gentlemen of the court, that is ridiculous! I am not the sort of man who disowns his writings, believe me: and indeed, among the documents presented by the public prosecutor— while I cannot recognize the Paterson newspaper—I fully recognize the pamphlet *Between Peasants* and the newspaper *L'Agitazione*. I am ready to argue with the public prosecutor on the basis of the pamphlet *Between Peasants* and the whole series of *L'Agitazione*, for which I claim full responsibility. First of all, though, let us not slander!

Mr. Presiding Judge, when a vile accusation was brought here and indignation wrung some colorful language out of me, you rightly enjoined me to regain my composure, since the accusation was not even deserving of my outrage.

Yet, Mr. Presiding Judge, did you notice that a much graver accusation came from the public prosecutor's seat? It was stated from there that anarchists are out to destroy the family! It never occurred to him that I might be outraged when one dares say that we have no family feelings. How did the public prosecutor prove that? I challenge him to find, in the entire history of the Inquisition in Spain, an argument such as he has employed to show that we do not countenance the family. What argument is that? "Malatesta says nothing about the family in the pamphlet *Between Peasants*. See, he says nothing about it because he is shrewd, because the peasants would have turned against such attacks on family feelings!" I need not labor the point that in that way one could prove whatever he wants: "Malatesta says nothing about parricide and rape. Malatesta is a sly fox! He is a parricide and a rapist precisely because he says nothing about parricide and rape!"

I wrote the pamphlet *Between Peasants* many years ago: it is only natural that it makes no mention of the family, because it was intended for the people and amid the people for whom there is no debate around the family; there is no point dealing with that issue amid the people, because everyone loves the family, because among the people there are no bourgeois who form families to get their hands on dowries.

Gentlemen of the court, I ask you to read that pamphlet, in which you can certainly find a dearth of ingenuity, but you will not be able to claim that its pages are not all ablaze with a blessed love of humanity.

Whoever uses that pamphlet to argue that we are against the family is slandering us. But there is more. From among the wealth of anarchist literature and my own writings, all the public prosecutor was able to find was a pamphlet and 40 newspaper issues. We can only assume, therefore, that he has studied his materials in depth, searching for what drives our cause.

How well were *L'Agitazione* articles about the family studied?

Let the public prosecutor read the article "*Emancipazione della donna*" and he will see what we think about the family. Besides, is there any need for written evidence in order to find out if we love the family? Ask the wives and children of these comrades, who weep in this courtroom or who, having been turned away by the guards, hover about this building like grieving shades! Look into these people's faces, and you will see these proud men change color at the merest reference to the family. I have no family myself, because my troubled life has not allowed me to form one; but I love my comrades' children as if they were my own and am loved by them in return. You would be convinced of that, had you seen my boy asking me with tears in his eyes not to speak, because he thought I might compromise myself by speaking out. Do you want human proof of what anarchists are about? That lad was brought by me to Italy because I wanted him to have a useful trade that might guarantee him a living and make him useful to himself and others. I have been arrested. The lad has found in Ancona as many mothers and fathers as there are families that love me.

Is this a party of malefactors?

The public prosecutor says that we want to destroy property. We are firm opponents of the institution of private property. Is that a crime, though? Are you to convict me, because I do not accept individual property? Cesare Beccaria, who was no inquisitor but a jurist—whom the public prosecutor will nevertheless acknowledge as no mean authority—Cesare Beccaria, whose effigy I saw on such an occasion as this in Rome, used to say that the property right is a terrifying thing. And do you know where I borrowed these ideas from, where I got to ponder the tormenting problems that afflict humanity? The writings of Filangieri, of Mario Pagano, the writings of all your philosophers, jurists, and economists. If you condemn me, you have to condemn all your history, all your glory.

I do not want to try your patience and shall not enter into a critique of private property. Strictly speaking, I would be entitled to do so, since the public prosecutor used our rejection of individual property to conclude that we are malefactors. I would have to muster up all the science of this century: you would not share my ideas, but you would agree that I am not a man to be countered by the policeman's handcuffs.

The public prosecutor says that we want to destroy society. Sure, we want to destroy the present social order. This morning, as I left prison, I had occasion to speak with some young boys you sure know, and after I asked them what they had done and encouraged them, do you know how they answered me? They answered: "That nitwit lawyer of ours has appealed. In here we eat every day and on Sundays they even serve beef." Mr. Presiding Judge, a society that, amid such development of mechanical and farming industry, such enlightenment from science, such rapidity of progress, cannot even ensure the necessities of life, well, that society is doomed to perish. However, the public prosecutor argues that I might be entitled perhaps to express all these ideas, if I did not seek to implement them with violence. Well, let us have a look at the sort of violence we want. I am a revolutionary because I believe that time is marching towards the full implementation of the present order's changeover. We believe that this transformation, after a period of preparation, will need violence. However, it is not due to us if the needs will be so urgent that the population will demand a changeover of the present order; we will only contribute to arouse those needs in the people, we will contribute to raise the popular consciousness.

And if you want to condemn us for spurring the people into revolution, then condemn all your schoolmasters, condemn your doctors and your hygienists, who teach the people about the need to wash and thus instill the need for soap in them. A man used to washing himself and aware of all the benefits of bodily cleanliness turns into a revolutionary the day he can no longer buy soap.

Let us come now to the matter of incitement. I am charged with being the leader of an association of malefactors. I shall not repeat all the counsels' arguments to prove to you that the criminal association does not exist. We are fellow members of the Social Studies Circle and there are four of us; even the basic requisite of the five members would be missing.[2] The public prosecutor says that I am the leader of the association. Not being able to prove that the crime exists, not being able to prove the association, he was not able to prove that I am its leader. Just because I happen to be a little better educated than my comrades, he labels me the leader and rewards me with extra months in custody, because I am the leader. He would need to show that these fellows obeyed my orders and that I insisted upon a double share of the loot. There is no criminal association where no sharing out of the loot has been agreed upon.

Now to incitement. The public prosecutor has done me a very great honor, an honor which, if rendered in earnest, would be enough to indemnify me for the three years of prison that he wants to give me: he said that since my arrival in Ancona, there has been a drop in murders, in thefts, and no more bombs have gone off. If this were true, then send me to prison, if you like, but you will send me there with a halo of glory. Yet am I to believe that a learned jurist should believe that, in a matter so complex as criminality, Malatesta's influence could be such a decisive influence?

Errico Malatesta is actually a poor exile who has spent ten months in Ancona—eight of which without any chance of acting effectively, and the other months he spent with the

2  The reference is to the least number of members required to recognize sufficient grounds for prosecution.

police on his trail. Is one to believe that the public prosecutor made that statement seriously? But I am beginning to think that the public prosecutor did make it seriously, when I compare that assertion with another one he made in order to send me to jail.

Neither my power to reduce crime nor my power to spark riots is true. Yet the public prosecutor reckons that if Malatesta could halt crime, he could equally spark riots. The shrewdness theory, for the public prosecutor, is a substitute for many things. He says that I understand that small deeds cannot lead to revolution, but I strive to avoid small revolutions so as to make big ones.

So be it, then. If I am no fool, though, why believe that I was foolish enough to believe that the revolution could be made, just because 200 women went out throwing stones? The public prosecutor says that I want to take advantage of popular discontent. Yes, I took advantage of it in Pietralacroce. You know what I did? You know what I do on every occasion that presents itself? In those moments in which the people's ears are opened, I try to slip through to them the ideas that on other occasions do not get through. Come the time when people's attention is drawn to some issue, I make myself heard to explain my ideas. When the price of bread soared, I went to Pietralacroce—and another ten places the police don't know about—I went there and I spoke to demonstrate that it is not by storming a cottage and stealing from a bakery that the social question can be resolved; I spoke up to say that if bread is expensive, it is not because the mayor is a scoundrel, not because [Antonio Starabba di] Rudinì (then Prime Minister of Italy) is a malefactor, but because of a whole series of social causes that can only be resolved through the organization of the masses, through the transformation of the property system.

I did what I would do tomorrow if a parricide or an infanticide occurred, in order to discuss the issue of the family.

The debate concerns incitement, and I claim that we acted as peacemakers. Read issue no. 40 of *L'Agitazione*, look at the article "Justice For All." That is how we incite to hatred; ask those mothers who came to thank us when their sons turned anarchist and stopped getting drunk, and became more loving sons and more diligent workers.

I see you are tired. If your conscience, rather than your interests, urges you to convict us, then go ahead and convict us. We will feel sorry for ourselves, because we love freedom, because we love to contribute to social activity; but we will feel sorrier for those who suffer on our behalf. Certainly, in the dismal hours in prison, when no one sees us, scorching tears may trickle from our eyes; then visions of women's melancholy and pale profiles, visions of children will make us cry. But we will endure it all, because we know that those who love us will be proud of us. I wish to the public prosecutor that his remorse may be soft, and I wish to you, should you convict us, that you may have the same peace of mind as we will have.

(*Repeated applause.* At various times, while Malatesta was speaking, sobbing was heard in the courtroom.)

MALATESTA WAS FOUND GUILTY, AND SENTENCED TO SEVEN months in prison. However, at the end of his sentence, he was not released, but sent to the penal colonies first at Ustica, followed by that at Lampedusa. But Malatesta would not be deterred, and escaped the island, landing first on Malta, and then making his way to London.

After his return to Italy years later, and following a massive wave of defeated factory occupations by Italian workers in 1920 (and subsequent rise in activity by Fascist gangs), Malatesta was once again arrested at the age of 67. However, he would wait more than six months in a cell without any charges being laid against him. Along with his comrades, he went on hunger strike to protest this treatment, finally being charged as part of a criminal conspiracy.

Gentlemen of the Court, Gentlemen of the jury!

Trials have always been one of our best means of propaganda and the dock has been the most efficient and, permit me to say it, the most glorious of our platforms. I should therefore not have lost the occasion to place before you a large exposition of the anarchist' program, maybe in the hope to convert one of yourselves to anarchism, encouraged in this by what happened to me at the *assizes* at Trani [trials for insurrections of August 1874—*ed.*]. Eleven of the jury not only acquitted me, but came, immediately to inscribe their names in the ranks of the International Workingmen's Association. But what shall I do? The public prosecutor, to whom I present my thanks and certify my admiration, did me a bad service: he cut the grass from underneath my feet. As matters stand now, if I made a great speech before you, I should resemble that old knight who, coated in steel, put on his best cuirass, lowered his ventail and jumped on the most fiery of his battle horses to ride in on the market to buy a pound of radishes!

I will say nothing further. I will only take advantage of the occasion to say something not in our interest, not in that of my comrades, but in the interest of the community, in the interest of that Italy which we are accused of not loving only because we wish it to be on terms of brotherhood with all other nations, only because besides loving the people of Italy, we love the people of all mankind, an internationalist and cosmopolitan conception, which by the way was at one time admitted and felt by all the fighters, all the heroes, all the martyrs of the Italian Resurrection who had overcome the limited idea of their native country and rushed into all parts of the globe to shed their blood on all the battlefields where a banner of freedom was raised.

You know that in Italy at this moment there is a war being waged which, by a singularity of our language is called a civil war, precisely because it is uncivil and savage. In Italy the situation is such we are returning to the dark and sanguinary night of the Middle Ages. Italy is full of mourning. Mothers, daughters, and wives are wailing, and why? Over a struggle without an aim. You know I am a revolutionist. I am for insurrection, I am also for violence when violence can serve a good cause. But blind violence, stupid violence, ferocious violence which today afflicts Italy—well, this is a sort of violence which must disappear; otherwise Italy will cease to be a civilized nation.

Gentlemen of the jury: You will give your verdict as your conscience will dictate you; to me it does not matter much; I am too hardened in the struggle to be impressioned by a little prison: if you bring in a verdict of guilt, I should say that you have committed judicial error, but I should not think that you have consciously committed a deliberate act of injustice. I should hold you in the same esteem, because I should be sure that your conscience dictated the verdict. But I am an optimist. I do not think that there are men who do evil for evil's sake, or if there exists such a man, he belongs more to the specialist in insanity than to the judge in criminal matters. But all the same, all do not think like myself. If you give a verdict of guilty, our friends, by party spirit, by overgreat affection for me, would interpret this as a class verdict, would interpret it as deliberate injustice, and you would have sown a new seed of hatred and rancor. Do not do this.

Gentlemen of the jury: This civil struggle is repugnant to all; it is repugnant to all by their elementary sense of common humanity, and then it is of no use to anybody, to none of the classes and parties, is of no use to the employers, the capitalists who need order for their industries and trades. It is not of any use to the proletarians who must work in order to live and who must prepare themselves for the elevation by practical experience and solidarity. It is not of any use to the conservatives who wish to conserve something other than ferocious massacre. It is of no use either to us who shall know to found upon the (present) hatred a harmonious society, a society of free men, the condition and guarantee of which shall be tolerance, the respect of honestly professed opinions. Send us home!

*(Clamorous applause quickly repressed by the presiding judge.)*

MALATESTA AND HIS COMRADES WERE ACQUITTED OF THE charges, and freed. Malatesta would continue to publish *Umanità Nova* until the following year, when it was suppressed by the new Fascist government. Malatesta died 11 years later, at the age of 78.

Marius
Jacob

**MARIUS JACOB 1905**

ALEXANDRE "MARIUS" JACOB WAS A FRENCH illegalist anarchist. After joining the merchant marines at the age of 12, and a brief stint as a pirate, Jacob rejected the life of work, and became a prolific thief. Jacob focused his robberies on social parasites like landlords, politicians, and members of the clergy. After pulling off more than 150 robberies, Jacob had an encounter with a cop that resulted in Jacob killing the cop. He was sentenced to hard labor in the prison colony of Cayenne, French Guiana. Jacob attempted escape from the courtroom by jumping from a skylight, but was immediately caught. He would attempt escape from Cayenne seventeen times, to no avail. He was finally released on December 30, 1928, at the age of 49.

---

You now know who I am: a rebel living off the products of his burglaries. In addition, I burned down several hotels and defended my freedom against the aggressions of the agents of power.

I laid bare to you my entire existence of combat: I submit it as a problem for your intellect.

Not recognizing anyone's right to judge me, I don't ask for either pardon or indulgence. I don't go begging to those I hate and hold in contempt. You are the stronger. Dispose of me as you wish; send me to a penal colony or the scaffold. I don't care! But before going our separate ways let me tell you one last thing.

Since you primarily condemn me for being a thief, it's useful to define what theft is.

In my opinion theft is a need that is felt by all men to take in order to satisfy their appetites. This need manifests itself in everything: from the stars that are born and die like beings, to the insect in space, so small, so infinite that our eyes can barely distinguish it. Life is nothing but theft and massacre. Plants and beasts devour each other in order to survive.

One is born only to serve as feed for the other. Despite the degree of civilization or, to phrase it better, perfectibility to which he has arrived, man is also subject to this law, and can only escape it under pain of death. He kills both plants and beasts to feed himself: he is insatiable.

Aside from objects of alimentation that assure him life, man also nourishes himself on air, water, and light. But have we ever seen two men kill each other for the sharing of these aliments? Not that I know of. Nevertheless these are the most precious of items, without which a man cannot live.

We can remain several days without absorbing the substances for which we make ourselves slaves. Can we do the same when it comes to air? Not even for a quarter of an hour. Water accounts for three quarters of our organism and is indispensable in maintaining the elasticity of our tissues. Without heat, without the sun, life would be completely impossible.

And so every man takes, steals his aliments. Do we accuse him of committing a crime? Of course not! Why then do we differentiate these from the rest? Because the rest demand the expending of effort, a certain amount of labor. But labor is the very essence of society; that is, the association of all individuals to conquer with little effort much well-being. Is this truly the image of what exists? Are your institutions based on such a mode of organization? The truth demonstrates the contrary.

The more a man works the less he earns. The less he produces the more he benefits. Merit is not taken into consideration. Only the bold take hold of power and hasten to legalize their rapine.

From top to bottom of the social scale everything is but dastardy on one side and idiocy on the other. How can you expect that penetrated with these truths I could have respected such a state of things?

A liquor seller and the boss of a brothel enrich themselves, while a man of genius dies of poverty in a hospital bed. The baker who bakes bread doesn't get any; the shoemaker who makes thousands of shoes shows his toes; the weaver who makes stocks of clothing doesn't have any to cover himself with; the bricklayer who builds castles and palaces wants for air in a filthy hovel. Those who produce everything have nothing, and those who produce nothing have everything.

Such a state of affairs can only produce antagonism between the laboring class and the owning, i.e., do-nothing, class. The fight breaks out and hatred delivers its blows.

You call a man a thief and bandit; you apply the rigor of the law against him without asking yourself if he could be something else. Have we ever seen a *rentier* [one who earns money through rental properties and/or investments—*ed.*] become a burglar? I admit that I've never known of this. But I, who am neither *rentier* nor landlord, I who am only a man who owns just his arms and his brains to ensure his preservation, had to conduct myself differently. Society only granted me three means of existence: work, begging, or theft. Work, far from being repugnant, pleases me: man cannot do without working. His muscles and brain possess a sum of energy that must be spent. What I hated was sweating blood and tears for a pittance of a salary; it was creating wealth that wouldn't be allowed me.

In a word, I found it repugnant to surrender to the prostitution of work. Begging is degradation, the negation of all dignity. Every man has a right to life's banquet.

*The right to live isn't begged for, it's taken.*

Theft is the restitution, the regaining of possession. Instead of being cloistered in a factory, like in a penal colony; instead of begging for what I had a right to, I preferred to rebel and fight my enemy face to face by making war on the rich, by attacking their goods.

Of course I understand that you would have preferred that I submit to your laws; that as a docile and worn out worker I would have created wealth in exchange for a miserable salary, and when my body would have been worn out and my brain softened I would have died on a street corner. Then you wouldn't have called me a "cynical bandit," but an "honest worker." Using flattery, you would even have given me the medal of labor. Priests promise paradise to their dupes. You are less abstract: you offer them a piece of paper.

I thank you for so much goodness, so much gratitude, messieurs. I'd prefer to be a cynic conscious of my rights instead of an automaton, a caryatid.

As soon as I took possession of my consciousness I gave myself over to theft without any scruples. I have no part in your so-called morality that advocates the respect of property as a virtue when in reality there are no worse thieves than landlords.

Consider yourselves lucky, messieurs, that this prejudice has taken root in the people, for this serves as your best gendarme. Knowing the powerlessness of the law, of force, to phrase it better, you have made them the most solid of your protectors.

But beware: everything only lasts a certain time. Everything that is constructed, built by ruse and force, can be demolished by ruse and force.

The people are evolving every day. Can't you see that having learned these truths, conscious of their rights, that all the starving, all the wretched, in a word: all your victims, are arming themselves with crowbars and assaulting your homes to take back the wealth they created and that you stole from them.

Do you think they'll be any more unhappy? I think the contrary. If they were to think carefully about this they would prefer to run all possible risks rather than fatten you while groaning in misery.

"Prison...penal colonies...the scaffold," it will be said. But what are these prospects in comparison with the life of a beast made up of all possible sufferings.

The miner who fights for his bread in the earth's entrails, never seeing the sun shine, can perish from one minute to the next, victim of an explosion; the roofer who wanders across the roofs can fall and be smashed to pieces; the sailor knows the day of his departure but doesn't know if he'll return to port. A good number of other workers contract fatal maladies in the exercise of their work, wear themselves out, poison themselves, kill themselves, to create for you. Even gendarmes and policemen—your valets—who, for the bone you give them to nibble on, sometimes meet death in the fight they undertake against your enemies.

Obstinate in your narrow egoism, do you not remain skeptical in regard to this vision? The people are frightened, you seem to be saying. We govern them through fear and repression. If he cries out we'll throw him in prison; if he stumbles we'll deport him to the penal colony; if he acts we'll guillotine him! All of this is poorly calculated, messieurs, believe you me. The sentences you inflict are not a remedy against acts of revolt. Repression, far from being a remedy, or even a palliative, is only an aggravation of the evil.

Collective punishment only plants hatred and vengeance. It's a fatal cycle. In any case, since you have been cutting off heads, since you have been populating the prisons and the penal colonies, have you prevented hatred from manifesting itself? Say something! Answer! The facts demonstrate your impotence.

For my part I knew full well that my conduct could have no other result than the penal colony or the scaffold. You must see that this did not prevent me from acting. If I gave myself over to theft it was not a question of gain, of lucre, but a question of principle, of right. I preferred to preserve my liberty, my independence, my dignity as a man rather than to make myself the artisan of someone else's fortune. To put it crudely, with no euphemisms: I preferred to rob rather than be robbed!

Of course I, too, condemn the act through which a man violently and through ruse takes possession of the fruits of someone else's labor. But it's precisely because of this that I made war on the rich, robbers of the poor. I too want to live in a society from which theft is banished. I only approved of and used theft as the means of revolt most appropriate for combating the most unjust of all thefts: individual property.

In order to destroy an effect you must first destroy the cause. If there is theft it is only because there is abundance on one hand and famine on the other; because *everything* only belongs to *some*. The struggle will only disappear when men will put their joys and suffering in common, their labors and their riches, when all will belong to everyone.

Revolutionary anarchist, I made my revolution.

*Vive l'anarchie!*

## RAYMOND CALLEMIN 1913

Raymond Callemin, known to his friends as Raymond la Science, was a member of the French anarchist illegalist group known as the Bonnot Gang. Callemin participated in numerous robberies, sometimes acting as getaway driver, in the world's first acts to utilize an automobile for this purpose. On April 7, 1912, at the age of 22, Callemin was arrested, but would have to await trial for almost a year.

Prior to their execution, some of Callemin's comrades-in-condemnation made a plea to the French president to spare their lives. Callemin refused to sign it. On his way to the guillotine, Callemin said "It's a day without a tomorrow...it's a fine thing, eh? The final agony of a man."

---

Every being comes into the world with a right to live a real life. This is indisputable, for it is nature's law. Also I ask myself why, on this earth, there are people who expect to have all the rights. They give the pretext that they have money, but if one asks them where they got their money from, what do they answer? As for myself, I answer as follows: "I give no one the right to impose his own wishes, regardless of the pretext given. I don't see whey I wouldn't have the right to eat those grapes or those apples just because they are the property of Mr. X.... What did he do that I have not that lets him alone gain an advantage? I answer nothing and consequently I have the right to make use of things according to my need and if he wants to prevent me forcibly I will revolt and against his strength I will oppose my own because, finding myself attacked, I will defend myself by any means at my disposal.

That's why, to those who will say that they have money and thus I must obey them, I will say: "When you are able to demonstrate that part of the whole represents the whole, that it is another earth than that on which you have been born, as I have, and that this is another sun the one which lights the way and makes plants grow and fruits ripen, when you have proven that, I will give you the right to keep me from living, because, well, where DOES money come from: from the earth, and silver is one part of the earth transformed into a metal that came to be called silver and one part of the world monopolized this silver and, in using this metal, violently forced the rest of the world to obey it. For this end, they invented all kinds of torture systems such as prisons, etc.

Why does this minority that "has" seem stronger than the majority that "has not"? Because this majority is ignorant and lacking in energy: it allows all sorts of caprices on the part of those who "have" by simply slouching its shoulders at each new caprice that comes up. Those people are too faint-hearted to revolt and moreover, if among them there are some who leave the flock, the others hold them back, either directly or indirectly, without knowing it but in just as dangerous a manner nonetheless. They claim honesty, but underneath that facade hides a hypocrisy and a cowardice that cannot be disavowed. From my earliest days, I knew the authority of the father and mother, and before I was even old enough to understand what it all meant I rebelled against that authority, just as I did against the authority of the educational system.

I was thirteen at the time. I started working; when I began to experience and understand what was going on around me. I also became familiar with life and social abuse; I saw people I found to be bad and corrupt, and told myself "I must find a way to get out of this shit of bosses, workers, bourgeoisie, judges, officers, and others; all of these people disgust me, some because they allow themselves to go through the motions of life without really doing a thing." Not wanting to be exploited or, on the other hand, be an exploiter of others, I stole from the shelves of stores, without getting too far ahead; the first time I was arrested I was seventeen; I was sentenced to three months in prison; and then I understood justice as it really was; my friend who was charged with the same crime (because we were working together) was given only two months, and that only a suspended sentence (of observation and good conduct). Why that was I have always wondered. But I can say that I give no one the right to judge me, be he a judge from the educational system or one from the tribunal, because no one can possibly understand or know the reasons for my actions; no one can put himself in my place, in a word, no one can be me. When I got out of prison, I returned to my parents, who reproached me severely. But to have undergone what I did in the name of "Justice," that is, prison, made me all the more rebellious. I started working again, although not the same job. (See, after having worked in an office for some time, I threw myself into work with a butcher, then into work in a deli, something which I did well, but now wherever I went people asked me for some sort of certification. I didn't have any, no one wanted to hire me, and that made me even more rebellious. That's when I began to play games in order to find work; I fixed up false certificates and finally found work for sixteen to eighteen hours a day for 70 to 80 francs a week, seven days a week, and when I asked for a day's vacation Monsieur the Boss got angry.

At the end of these months of work there, I was distraught and exhausted and yet I had to keep going for fear of dying of hunger, seeing that what I earned was just enough to pay for my most basic needs, but to look at what was going on the other side of the street, I felt that my boss was reaping all the benefits of my work and what was he doing to deserve that? Nothing, other than reminding me that I had arrived ten minutes late or criticizing my work and threatening me with losing my job if my work didn't improve.

Anyway, as I don't like doing the same thing all the time (I don't think of myself as a machine), I would have liked to teach myself, to know lots of things, to develop my intelligence as well as my body, in a word to become a being capable of moving out in all directions as he pleases, needing as little as possible from others around him. But to get to that point, I needed time, I needed books. How could I get those things while remaining so tied to my work? It was impossible for me to pull these things together as I had to eat and in order to do that I had to work and for whom? For a boss. I thought all this over and said for myself: I am going to change jobs once again, maybe things will go better for me now, but I really hadn't expected to encounter a social system like the one I find myself fighting constantly these days; I was pretty interested in mechanical work, but when I inquired about working, mechanics responded: We'd like to take you on but we can't pay you because you wouldn't work fast enough since you don't know anything about what it takes to be a mechanic... They would (one day) pay me, but only once I knew the rudiments of the trade, which meant in fifteen to eighteen months (or more) and then they could pay me six to eight francs a day for ten to twelve hours of work per day. The state really began to disgust me at this point. In the end I found work digging embankments but nothing changed: I had to work a lot in order to fall short of satisfying even my most basic needs. I came to the same conclusions in looking at situations all around me; I saw nothing but poverty for those who worked at my side and, worse, all these miserable people, instead of trying to get out of the rut they were in, dug in their heels and drank themselves into oblivion, thereby casting their faculties of reason to the wind.

I saw all that, I saw the exploiter getting satisfied by the whole thing, and worse, I saw him pay for rounds of drinks for men who had already drunk too much; and for good reason, for while they got drunk, the workers couldn't think, and that's what was necessary to keep them under the authority of the exploiting bosses.

When, accidentally, there was a gesture of revolt by the imbeciles (I make no distinction by trade here), the bosses threatened to fire them and the imbeciles calmed down immediately.

I went on strike once too, but I quickly understood the meaning and the ramifications of this token gesture. All of those "men," incapable of acting individually, appointed a leader whose responsibility it was to discuss the discontent among our members with the boss.

Sometimes this stupid leader sold out to the boss by asking for a small bribe, whereas when the other brutes had no money he suggested they return to work if they needed to pay for things. These were the results, the rewards we got from the strikes, and when we did finally get a raise, the capitalists reacted by increasing the cost of our food, so much so that nothing really changed, we had lost a lot of time and energy, that's all. Also, in the unions, I only made one short appearance, as I was quickly aware that all of these gentlemen were nothing more than profiteers and careerists who screamed for rebellion everywhere, but why? I understood that they wanted

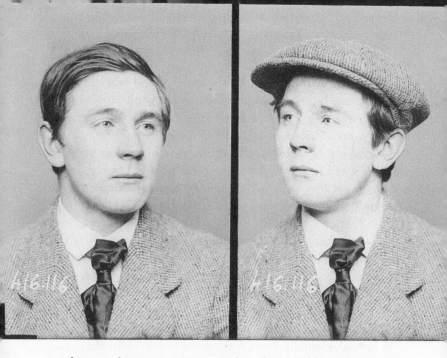

to destroy the present state so that they could put themselves in power, to change the whole apparatus in name only. Like the capitalists, they utilized the same technique: promises. One's sincerity, in the end, is only one more lousy working class trait to be exploited. When I left this, I came upon a group that was somewhat different: the revolutionaries. I then became an anarchist. I was eighteen, I didn't want to return to work, and I started my campaign of individual reprisals once again, with the same unfortunate luck as before. After three or four months, I was arrested.

I was sentenced to two months' imprisonment. When I got out I tried to find work. I worked on a general strike, during which we had a lot of trouble with the police. I was arrested and sentenced to six days in jail.

All of this sharpened my character and, naturally, the more I learned, the more I understood about life. I spent time with anarchists, I understood their theories and became a fervent supporter of their point of view, not because the theories seemed good but because I found them to be the most just of those that were current at the time.

In the anarchist milieu I encountered individuals who were trying as much as possible to get rid of their prejudices, those same prejudices that made this world so stupid and savage, people with whom I enjoyed talking because they showed me things I could see and touch rather than utopias. More than that, these people were sober, clear thinkers. When with them I didn't have to turn my head the other way as I did with most of the brutes, their mouths didn't reek of alcohol or tobacco. They seemed reasonable and I found them to have lots of energy and iron wills.

My opinions solidified, I became a part of the group, I wanted no part of the world in which I worked for others, I wanted to work for myself, but in order to do that, I didn't have much choice, but I had acquired some experience in some areas, and, full of energy myself, I resolved to defend myself to the death against the stupid yelping of the present society.

I left Paris when I was nineteen and a half, because I saw that everything in the city was becoming regimented. I understood what the words republic, liberty, equality, fraternity, flag, country and so on meant. I mulled these words over, what part was I to take in all of this and I also spoke with my friends about the supposed valor of that social vocabulary that surrounded me; I understood the horrible hypocrisy represented by the language of the state. It's all nothing more than a religion, like God's religion that gets slopped out to the world's religious folk. They say to them, "respect your country, die for your country," but what is the nation for me, it's all the earth without borders. "Country" is where I like, whether it is in Germany, Russia, or France, for me "country" or "nation" knows no bounds, it is everywhere that I am contented. I don't distinguish between peoples, I seek only mutual understanding, but around me I see only religious types and

Christians or deceitful hypocrites. If the workers would think a bit, they would see and understand that between capitalists there are no boundaries, these rapacious wrongdoers organize themselves to oppress others better. It is only now that I am here and it is now that I must live and I shall do just that by any means that science puts at my disposal. I may not like to be terribly old, I will probably be overtaken by the open struggle between me and the society which has better means of winning than I will ever have, but I will defend myself as best I can; to deceitfulness and trickery I will respond in kind, likewise to force, until I am beaten, which is to say dead.

Around May of 1910 I tried to go to the provinces, hoping to leave the country and thereby escape military service, but in July I was put in prison for assault and battery. I got out at the end of August, one month before my class of military trainees was to leave. As soon as I left prison, I got a job with a ditch-digging concern to earn some money; I took the train for the Belgian border, paying for part of the trip, but not all of it—I had to have money to eat on the train. Once in Valenciennes, I got off the train, looked for the exit doors of the station, and was spied on by a policeman, who asked me a few questions, then let me go. I didn't have any money, so I took a job for a week. I committed two robberies and left the country for Belgium. I got to Charleroi around the sixth of October, found a job for a few days, got to know a group of anarchists, and in the early part of November I was arrested and then released eight days later (they couldn't prove the charges against me).

I worked for a bit, met some people with similar opinions, people who were frank, motivated, with whom I did some robberies. I was twenty and a half years old.

February 1911. I had to get out of Brussels as they were looking to accuse me of doing those robberies at Charleroi; I returned to Paris, where I worked on the newspaper Anarchy, something I worked hard for. I worked hard, just about every day of the week, and as usual I was a bit thin, so I did a couple of robberies without much real success. I started printing counterfeit bills, but that wasn't too successful and it was just as risky as doing a big job that would bring in more money. I stopped the counterfeiting.

In July, lots of my friends were arrested. I was upset and determined to avenge my position in this criminal society. I left the newspaper and moved to Vincennes with some friends.

While working on the newspaper, we decided to rent a number of rooms so as to better insure our security. We didn't have much money so we robbed some places to get what we needed.

For a time I had been looking for a friend to drive me places, but I couldn't find anyone. I had learned to drive but, not being very skillful at it, I was hesitant to try stealing a car and risk causing our group more trouble than we could handle. It was during this time that I met [Jules] Bonnot.

It was about December 10, 1911, at night, that we stole a car in Boulonge and proceeded to hide it in a friend's garage. I told him simply that we would be back for it in eight hours or so. I gave him a false name and false address and we left.

We discussed what we had to do. We had two big jobs to do. We were four strong. We drove around Paris for the rest of the night until 8:30 the next morning. I stayed at the wheel and grew confident in my own abilities to handle the curves in the road, even at high speed. That was good, we really needed two drivers in case one was wounded in the pursuit.

At 8:30 I let Bonnot take over.

We hadn't mutually decided how we were to pull off what we wanted to do—rob a cash collector. We had already observed the collector and timed his arrival at the rue Ordineur but still, it was nine in the morning, right out in the middle of the street, and in a quarter which was rather heavily populated.

At 9:00 exactly we spotted him stepping off the street car as usual, accompanied by someone else assigned to protect him. We don't have a second to lose; the car approaches him, I get out, hand on my revolver. My companion on the other side of the sidewalk is a few steps behind me.

Three feet away from the cashier, I take out my revolver, coldly, and shoot him twice; he falls, his accompanying guard runs off; I pick up one sack, my companion takes another.

We get back in the car, some passerby trying to keep us from getting in. We pull out our revolvers, shoot, and everyone flees. We take the route to Le Havre, taking lots of detours to keep from getting caught or having to put up a fight (we aren't poorly armed). I have no less than six revolvers on my person. We had about four hundred rounds and had decided to fight to the death if we had to.

We were hungry. I let Bonnot drive. Later, we started running out of gas and decided to leave the car behind, having arrived at the sea and the sandy earth pulling our tires down into it. We throw the license plates away. We get to the train station to get tickets to Paris and arrive without incident, though the national security agency is close at our feet. I expect they thought the revolution had begun? To think that it was only a slightly serious prank. They are going to see quite a few more before they fall...

## ENRIQUE FLORES MAGÓN 1916

ENRIQUE FLORES MAGÓN WAS THE BROTHER OF the more well known Ricardo Flores Magón. Together they were jailed at least twice in Mexico for their writings and actions, before leaving Mexico for the United States, where they resumed publication of their newspaper *Regeneración*. They would find as much luck in the US, where they would serve three jail sentences each for their published words.

In what would be the brothers' second US trial, a grand jury indicted the Magón brothers on February 18, 1916 for violation of Comstock Laws which prohibited using the postal service to mail materials that the government deemed "obscene". Included in this was material "tending to incite arson, murder, or assassination." The Magón brothers' crime consisted of mailing an issue of *Regeneración* that contained a passage that read

> "The ones who should be shot are the [Texas] "rangers" and the band or bandits who accompany them in their depredations. Enough of reforms!...Down with the so-called rights of private property, and as long as this evil right continues

> to exist, we shall continue under arms...Poor peo-
> ple, whoever speaks to you about *Carranzismo*,
> spit in their face and break their jaw. Long live
> land and liberty!"

Enrique resisted his arrest, and was rewarded with a half-dozen stitches. Despite the following statement by Enrique, he was ultimately sentenced to pay a $1000 fine, and serve three years in prison. His brother Ricardo, who was in very poor health, fighting diabetes, received a one-year sentence along with his $1000 fine.

-------------------

On account of my brother's sickness, which prevents his addressing this Court, I shall speak in his behalf as well as my own. I am taking the opportunity given me of addressing the Court because I want to make clear the causes behind our prosecution, for it appears that Court procedure was designed to conceal the facts underlying such cases as this.

The records of this trial show that the Magón brothers were tried and convicted, but the records do not show that the case at bar here is the age-long fight of the downtrodden and the disinherited against the tyranny, the superstition and the oppression which overburdens mankind.

It is not merely the Magóns who are convicted in this Court, but all liberty and justice loving people; for we, the Magón brothers, have been convicted by the technicalities of man-made laws, for our activities in behalf of the emancipation of the downtrodden, particularly of the Mexican proletarians, and of the disinherited all over the world in general, as shown by our writings, which are a part of the record of this case.

With the Magóns you have convicted the world's red-blooded

men and women who are striving to halt the piracy and the oppression of the rapacious plutocracy and its natural allies, Authority and the Church. With us you have condemned all of the men and women who think and who feel the anguish and the sorrows of the dispossessed, the tortures of the oppressed, the wailing and the tears of the millions of human beings who have the misfortune of being born at a time when all of the means of life have been appropriated by the land-sharks and the money-grabbers of the millions of proletarians who are condemned at birth to a life of incessant toil and actual chattel slavery, without hope of any reward other than slow death from starvation and exposure.

After studying these conditions many men and women have come to the conclusion that the only way out of this slavery is the way we pointed out in our Manifesto of September 23rd, 1911. As we set forth in that document, we aim to establish the common ownership of the land, of the machinery and the means of production and distribution, for the common use and benefit of all human beings, so as to enable them to work and earn their own living and to enjoy the honest pleasures which nature intended for them.

These ideals are destructive to the present institutions, as properly remarked here by the prosecution and this Court, and are, therefore, antagonistic to man-made laws that uphold Capitalism, but this does not mean that they are not founded on sound principles of Justice and Freedom.

We are asked what we have to say why sentence should not be passed on us. This Court should not pass sentence on us, for it would mean to deny to us Mexican people the perfect right we have to revolt against the unbearable conditions that have kept us in slavery through long, long years; conditions under which we found ourselves stripped of all our belongings, our lands, our forests, our rivers, our mines and everything else that we once owned in common or individually since time immemorial. We saw all our belongings being taken from us by Porfirio Díaz by means of violence through his soldiery and legal machinery. Díaz robbed the Mexican people in order that he might grant concessions to the Otises, Hearsts, Rockefellers, Morgans, Guggenheims, Pearsons and other foreign interests. And these concessions were granted for a mere song in order to perpetuate the Díaz regime.

After we were dispossessed of our natural heritage, we found ourselves held in bondage, in real chattel-slavery, forced to work our own lands, lands that were now no longer ours; we were forced to work sixteen and eighteen hours a day for from $.18 to $.37 Mexican money, that is equal to from $.9 to $.18 American money. We were compelled to trade with the "tienda de raya," which is the same as the commis- saries of your mining and lumber camps, where everything was sold to us at exorbitant prices. Under such conditions we gradually found ourselves in perpetual debt to our masters and without the liberty of moving from their domain. In case we succeeded in evading the vigilance of the hacienda bosses and escaped from our bondage, we were caught by the authorities and once more returned to slavery.

Whenever we went on strike for better conditions and wages, as in Rio Blanco and Cananea, we were shot down en masse by the trained murderers of Díaz, his soldiers, his police-men and rangers. If we still held a small piece of land that excited the greed of the authorities, the rich or the clergy, it was taken from us by hook or crook. They even resorted to cold-blooded murder.

Our freedom was trampled upon. Our speakers were arrested and shot in the dark of the night. Our papers were suppressed and the writers imprisoned, often vanishing from the face of the earth. Many of our brothers who still believed in the ballot met their death in front of the polls at the hands of the Díaz soldiers. Many of our brothers were sold for $200 per head to the slave drivers of Yucatan and the Valle Nacional. They were sold into actual slavery and there forced to work under such horrible conditions that their health was soon broken, and when they no longer could stand on their feet they were often buried alive in order to save bother and medical expenses. It was a common sight to see our brothers beaten to death for the slightest provocation.

We endured these conditions for thirty-six years, which proves that we are a peace-loving people. But we found ourselves so cornered and driven against the wall, that we finally had to revolt against damnable conditions in order to save ourselves and to gain Bread, Land and Liberty for All.

This was the cause and the source of the Social and Economic Revolution which has for over five years shaken Mexico; the revolution of the downtrodden masses against their oppressors and exploiters; the revolution that chiefly aims to get control in common of the land and, thereby aims to free the Mexican people. These purposes and aspirations are set forth in condensed form in our battle cry of "Land and Liberty!"

We Mexicans are striving to get back the land, because we know that the land is the source of all social wealth and, therefore, that he who owns the land owns all and, hence, becomes economically free. A people who enjoy economic freedom are free socially and politically as well; that is to say, economic freedom is the mother of all freedom.

Against the outrageous conditions that I have here roughly outlined, we Mexicans revolted; and now two of us, Ricardo and myself, are facing sentence here for our activity in that rebellion and for striking to gain our political, social and economic emancipation.

We therefore think that, as a principle of justice, this Court should not impose a sentence on us; for such a sentence would mean a flat denial that the Mexican people have a right to fight their own battles and to fight them in their own way.

Our revolutionary methods may not meet with the approval of the "peace at any price" gentlemen, but they have the sanction of Thomas Jefferson, who said: "We cannot expect to pass from Despotism to Liberty on a feather bed."

The institutions springing from private property are the source and cause of all slavery, vice and crime. It is on account of private property that a large majority of human beings are slaves; producing all the wealth, they go destitute. It is on account of private property, which deprives men and women of the just reward of their labor, that our women prostitute themselves, our children grow weak and consumptive in the mills of Capitalism, our men become drunkards, dope fiends, thieves, suicides, insane and murderers.

That is why we hate private property and fight for its abolition and strive to implant Communist anarchism wherein the land, the machinery and all the means of production and transportation shall be owned in common, so that all may have an equal chance for life, liberty and the pursuit of happiness; so that all being supplied in their needs and on an equal social, political and economic standing, ignorance, vice and crime shall vanish, naturally and automatically for their source, private property, will have been abolished forever.

We are opposed to the church for the reason heretofore given; it upholds the evil called private property and keeps submerged in ignorance and superstition the human mind.

We are opposed to government because it is the staunch upholder of private property and because government means imposition, tyranny, oppression and violence. We agree with Thomas Jefferson when he says: "History in general informs us how bad government is." While quoting Jefferson, I should like to remark that he was twice President of the United States, and, therefore, he knew what he was talking about. And on the 12th of this month, this court agreed with us when it said, "It is the duty of government to preserve itself." That means that government is not "of the people, by the people and for the people," but that it is in fact an institution alien to the people, and against whose interests it shall preserve itself. And we are duly grateful to this court for that acknowledgment.

Striving as we are through our revolutionary activities to gain justice, freedom, plenty and happiness for all human beings, we believe that, as a matter of justice this court has no right to impose a sentence on us. You may have the power, but you have not the right to do so.

The prosecution charged us with inciting to revolution in this country. The charge is baseless as well as illogical. Revolutions cannot be incited.

I have often compared the present conditions in this country with the conditions which confronted the Mexican people under the Díaz regime, and I have found them very similar in many instances. The American workingmen, as a whole, are often forced to work at wages on which no man can decently live, just as the Mexican peons were forced to do.

The lumber camps of Louisiana, the mines of Colorado and West Virginia and other places are practically the same as the hellholes of Yucatan and the Valle Nacional. Here also you have the "commissary" which is the counterpart of our "tienda de raya." Our massacres of Rio Blanco and Cananea have their parallel in Ludlow, Coeur D'Alene and West Virginia. The suppression of our papers by Díaz is similar to the suppression here of The Woman Rebel, Revolt, The Alarm, Voluntad, The Blast, and finally, our Regeneración. Free speech, free assemblage and free press, as well as freedom of thought, are dealt with in this country a la Porfirio Díaz.

On the other hand, you have here, as reported by the commission of industrial relations, 5 percent of the population owning 65 percent of the wealth, just as we had in Mexico. And as in Mexico, the multitude of producers are living either in pauperism or very close to actual want.

Here, too, you have your large landowners, and the number of your tenant farmers is ever increasing. American people, as the Mexican, are learning that the very earth under their feet has been taken away by the land-sharks and by huge land grants to special interests. Your mines and your forests are going the same way into the same hands that the mines and forests of Mexico went. The liberties of the American people have gradually been encroached upon just as they were in Mexico.

As like causes produce like results, it does not require a great deal of wisdom to see the trend of events of this country. Revolution is breeding, but it is coming from "above" and not from the workers, for it is only when the conditions of the proletariat become unbearable that they rise in revolt.

Unless present conditions change, you American people of the present generations will have to face the bloodiest revolution in the annals of history.

Jefferson, who was the anarchist of his time, and who is acknowledged as a great patriot and thinker, saw the necessity of revolution and justified its drastic measures. He said, "I hold that a little rebellion now and then is a good thing, and as necessary in the political world as storms in the physical." At another time he said, "The spirit of resistance is so valuable on certain occasions that I wish it always to be kept alive." And once more hear what Jefferson said: "Let these [the people] take arms. What signify a few lives in a century or two? The tree of liberty must be refreshed from time to time with the blood of patriots and tyrants. It is its natural manure."

In answer to the able argument for a new trial, made on the 12th of this month by our honest and courageous counsel, Mr. Ryckman, the Court said: "These men have no right to seek refuge in this country." We hold that we do have such right, not only as a principle of justice and civilization, but your Constitution specifically grants us the right of asylum as political refugees.

Jefferson, Paine, and Franklin, during the American Revolution, not only acted as agents of the American rebels in France, but they actually secured the assistance of France in their revolt against England. From this we can see that one hundred and fifty years ago the French people recognized a principle of humanity which this court now denies us.

The court has spoken of us as aliens to this country and its people. The court is in error. We are aliens to no country, nor are we aliens to any people on earth. The world is our country and all men are our countrymen. It is true that, by birth, we are Mexicans, but our minds are not so narrow, our vision not so pitifully small as to regard as aliens or enemies those who have been born under other skies.

The court suggested that it would be more becoming for us to go to Mexico to shoulder a musket and fight for our rights. If the Mexican revolution were an attempt of one set of politicians to oust or overthrow another set of office-holders, then the court's suggestion would be very apt. The revolution in Mexico is, however, not a political but a social and economic revolution and it is necessary to educate people, to teach them the real causes of their misery and slavery, and to point out to them the way to freedom, fraternity and equality.

This is why our hands, instead of being armed with muskets are armed with pens; a weapon more formidable and far more feared by tyrants and exploiters. I believe that it was Emerson who said that "Whenever a thinker is turned loose, tyrants tremble." And it is because it is acknowledged that we are thinkers as well as fighters, that we have spent over seven years out of the twelve that we have been here in the jails and prisons of the land of the "free."

We are not asking the court for mercy; we are demanding justice. If, however, this court is to be actuated by man-made laws instead of fundamental justice and, therefore, insists on sending us to the penitentiary, you may do so without hesitation.

A penitentiary sentence to us will likely mean our graves, for we are both sick men. We alone know how our health has been undermined. We know that another penitentiary sentence, no matter how light it may be, will be a death sentence. We feel that we shall not come out of the penitentiary alive.

However, it does not matter to us personally; from the beginning of our struggle, twenty-four years ago, we dedicated our lives to the cause of freedom. Since that time we have suffered a long chain of persecution and conspiracy, of which this case is but another link, but we still hold to our original purpose of doing our duty to our fellowmen, no matter what the result to us personally.

History is watching us from her throne, and she is registering in her annals the social drama that is now being enacted in this court. We appeal to her with a clean conscience, and with our hearts normally beating and with our brains dreaming of a future society, wherein there will be happiness, freedom and justice for all mankind.

The court may choose between law and justice. If you send us to our graves and brand us once more with the stigma of felons, we are sure that history will reverse the sentence. She will mark indelibly the forehead of the Cain.

*Let the Court speak! History watches!*

**MOLLIE STEIMER 1918**

IN 1918, MOLLIE STEIMER STOOD TRIAL (WITH three other members of the *Frayhayt* publishing collective) for campaigning against US military involvement in the Russian Civil War. The whole of their illegal act was to distribute leaflets. While out on bail, Steimer was arrested at least eight more times, usually without charge, but at least once she was charged with inciting a riot. She was eventually convicted under the Espionage Act and sentenced to fifteen years in prison, *for distributing leaflets*. In 1921, an immigration court ruled that she should be deported back to her native Russia. But the deportation couldn't take place immediately, because Steimer first refused to leave her cell until all political prisoners were free, and then refused to be transported by train because of a railroad strike that was in progress. She refused to be transported by scabs.

Steimer and her comrades arrived in Russia after Emma Goldman and Alexander Berkman's disillusionment with the "revolution," after both the Kronstadt rebellion and Nestor Makhno's insurgent army had been suppressed by the Bosheviks. Despite her disappointment, Steimer did have the opportunity to meet Senya Fleshin, who would become her lifelong partner, who had also been deported from the US for his anarchist activity. After multiple arrests (and a sentence in Siberia), Steimer and Fleshin were soon deported to Germany.

> "Victims of the Red Scare in America, they be-
> came victims of the Red Terror in Russia."
>
> —Paul Avrich, *Anarchist Portraits*

---

When asked by the judge if she was an anarchist, Steimer declared:

By anarchism, I understand a new social order, where no group of people shall be governed by another group of people. Individual freedom shall prevail in the full sense of the word. Private ownership shall be abolished. Every person shall have an equal opportunity to develop himself well, both mentally and physically. We shall not have to struggle for our daily existence as we do now. No one shall live on the product of others. Every person shall produce as much as he can, and enjoy as much as he needs—receive according to his need. Instead of striving to get money, we shall strive towards education, towards knowledge. While at present the people of the world are divided into various groups, calling themselves nations, while one nation defies another—in most cases considers the others as competitive—we, the workers of the world, shall stretch out our hands towards each other with brotherly love. To the fulfillment of this idea I shall devote all my energy, and, if necessary, render my life for it.

Upon sentencing, Steimer stated:

I do not believe in any authorities, but what I do want to say is this, that though you have sent military troops to Russia to crush the Russian Revolution, though you may succeed in slaughtering hundreds of thousands of revolutionists, you will by no means succeed in subduing the revolutionary spirit. On the contrary, the more you will seek to suppress the truth, the sooner will the thought of truth and light enter the hearts of the workers and the sooner is the international social revolution bound to come.

As far as the charges against me are concerned, I am responsibly for my deeds and ready to stand the consequences, no matter what they may be.

*For Freedom,*
*Louise Olivereau.*
*Cañon City Colo 11-21-18*

**LOUISE OLIVEREAU 1918**

IN 1917, FOUR MONTHS AFTER US ENTRY INTO World War I, Louise Olivereau, a stenographer working for the Seattle IWW, printed circulars questioning the newly instituted military draft. She mailed over 2,000 of these appeals to conscientious objection to men that had been drafted. One copy made it's way to the Postmaster, and then to the Department of Justice. Federal agents raided the Seattle offices of the IWW, and confiscated copies of the circular, as well as books that Olivereau had received in the mail. Olivereau decided to try to retrieve her property from the feds, and went to their offices, where they questioned her about the circular, and then escorted her to her home to retrieve more copies of it. There, they arrested her, charging her with violation of the recently passed Espionage Act, which made it illegal to encourage resistance to the military draft. She was then transported to Pierce County Jail in Tacoma, with a $7500 bail. Olivereau would spend three months in this jail awaiting trial and judgment.

At trial, she chose to go without a lawyer, stating that a lawyer "would worry more over getting me a light sentence than over the preservation of the ideals I care for more than for my own liberty." She attempted to filter out prospective jurors that had prejudice against anarchists, or believed that people didn't have a right to free speech during wartime, but her attempts were stifled by the judge. Ultimately her jury was not made up of her peers, but included a retired banker, a real estate broker, a wealthy hardware merchant, and a man with seven sons serving in the military.

Like any true Manichean, the judge responded to Olivereau's discussions of the war by declaring that "the time for a discussion of the merits of the war is past. There are only two sides to the war. One side is in favor of the United States; the other side is in favor of the enemies of this country."

Following Olivereau's speech, the jury deliberated for a mere 30 minutes before declaring her guilty of three counts of "attempting to cause insubordination, disloyalty, mutiny and refusal of duty in the military," and three of "unlawfully using the mails and postal service of the United States for transmission of unmailable matter." The judge sentenced her to 75 total years, but deemed the many sentences should be served concurrently, adding up to 10 years, and declared that people like Olivereau "strike at the very foundation of the Government and outrage the feelings of true Americans..."

Olivereau's friend, Minnie Parkhurst, attempted to raise funds for an appeal, but the IWW and other comrades deemed the cause less important than other higher profile trials at the time, and also publicly emphasized that Olivereau was an *employee* of the IWW, not a *member*, in an attempt to distance themselves from her. All this came after she spent portions of her trial defending the IWW. Olivereau was also ultimately abandoned by her friend Anna Louise Strong, who had seen political repercussions due to their friendship.

Ultimately, Olivereau served twenty-eight months of her sentence before being released.

May it please your Honor and Gentlemen of the jury: I find myself just a little bit overwhelmed by the oratory you have just listened to. If it takes me a little time to recover you will, I know, be patient. I have explained to you before that this is my first appearance in a Court of Law; not only that, but the circumstances of the case make it difficult to conduct it along the lines which might seem easiest and most desirable. I have never been a public propagandist in Seattle, and to a very limited extent only in any other place; therefore it is impossible for me to produce witnesses or evidence to the effect that it was not my habit to advocate lawbreaking either forcibly or by any other means, to bring about any social change that I might consider desirable. The prosecution has not been able to establish either through its witnesses or by any evidence that it has introduced that I have ever at any time advocated forcible resistance to the draft law. The circulars themselves speak eloquently in denial of any suggestions that I would urge conscripts or any one else to make forcible resistance to the draft law. There are suggestions of violence or force contained in some of those circulars. Those suggestions for violence are not from me but are copied from a speech made by Elihu Root, who is lauded as a patriotic and loyal supporter of the administration. What I have done, and what I purposed to do, in the sending out of these circulars was to call attention of drafted men to the fact that they are asked, or rather ordered, to resign their right to think for themselves or the right to judge for themselves what was the best good of the country and what that good demanded in their relation to a question on which they had been given no opportunity to vote; the right to dispose of their own lives, and incidentally, of the lives of others dependent upon them or other wise closely connected with them, in the manner which might seem to them to the best advantage of all concerned. A very large part of the matter contained in these circulars is copied from books which may be found upon the shelves of the Public Library. The rest is frank discussion by a Conscientious Objector with men who may or may not be like-minded, but who certainly have a right and an interest in knowing the position of such Conscientious Objector.

Because I have not been a public propagandist, and can not refer you to past public utterances on the subject of war and government, and because I was not allowed to develop what my views as an Anarchist really are on these points, in my examination of the jury, it becomes necessary for me now, in order to establish motive, to set forth in some detail just what I do believe, and why, and the circumstances which caused me to write and send these circulars. First, let me very briefly review the facts of the arrest and attendant circumstances.

You have been informed that I went to Mr. Wright's office on the morning of Sept. 7 to regain possession, if possible, of certain books belonging to me personally, which were confiscated in the raid on the I. W. W. office at 40 Union Block, Sept. 5. After some discussion, Mr. Wright stated it as his opinion that the books would doubtless be returned to me, since the purpose of the raid did not include the holding of any property other than that belonging to the I. W. W. I have not as yet received the books.

The burden of Mr. Wright's questions concerning the circulars which he showed me in his office, was, how many had been prepared in and mailed from 40 Union Block; whether I had prepared them there; whether the work had been done on typewriters or mimeographs belonging to the organization, etc.; all of which I was able to answer truthfully in the negative, since nothing of the matter was known to anyone in the office, nor had any of the work been done there.

I had known that the letter to Mr. Leach, in Bellingham, had come to the knowledge of the post office authorities, a very few days after it was written. Allow me to point out that that letter contained one of the alleged seditious circulars, and yet it was delivered to Mr. Leach with the full knowledge of its character, by the post office officials. Knowing that the government was fully aware of what I was doing, and could stop me at any time if they wished, I continued to prepare and send out my circulars, and was not arrested until more than a week after the last lot was mailed. Judging from the persistent effort made by Mr. Wright, Mr. Allen and Mr. Perkins to connect these circulars with the work of the I. W. W. I can only conclude that my arrest was delayed until after the raid in the hope that such a connection could be established.

In a discussion, lasting something like two hours, I quite frankly stated my views on patriotism, violence, obedience to law, and other related subjects, to Mr. Allen, Mr. Wright and Mr. Perkins. My opinions on these matters have never been a secret, though I have not shouted them from the housetops. I have governed my life in accordance with these principles, and never before have they brought me in conflict with the laws of this country. I do not believe they have now brought me in conflict with the law, though they have brought me in conflict with what appears to be, for the time, the governing force of the country. Though Mr. Allen stated that he was uncertain whether I was a harmless sentimentalist or a dangerous woman, it was decided safest to take no risk, and I was held for arrest.

During the progress of the case you have had some opportunity to learn what the philosophy of Anarchism is. In order to refresh your minds as to the points which have been developed, and to connect those points into a coherent whole, let me make a short statement of what this philosophy actually is.

The word itself is from the Greek word 'arche', meaning force, power or violence, and 'an' , without. Anarchy, then is a condition without force or violence. Anarchism is the working philosophy of those who desire to bring about a condition of society in which force and violence will have no place. As a social student, I am convinced that violence breeds violence, war breeds hatreds and fears and revengeful desires which lead to other wars; suppression within a nation or a community results in rebellion, insurrection, revolution. A thoughtful survey of the evolution of life, whether from the point of view of physical or social development, leads inevitably to the conclusion that mutual aid, the communal sense, the social sense, recognition of common interest among individuals, is the greatest factor in the world's progress, and always has been. Struggle for supremacy between individuals, between tribes, between nations, is a reactionary, destructive force. It wastes energy; it wastes time; it separates and embitters the individuals or nations engaging in such struggle; it prevents progress along constructive lines in any direction.

One of the fundamental necessities for progress in any society is perfect freedom of discussion, and another is perfect freedom of experiment, with various forms of social organization, laws, or other measures connected with community or national life. Ideas occur to single individuals oftener than to masses of people; therefore the right of minorities to propagate their ideas must be inviolate if we are to have a progressive society. In most matters, it is right that the majority should determine the policy of a nation; in almost none is it safe or advisable, for the peace and progress of the nation, for the majority to compel the minority to conform to the will of the majority, or to silence the minority or in any way prevent it from attempting to make itself a majority.

These principles are recognized not only by Anarchists as essential to the fullest and most beneficial development of individuals and nations, but our own government is theoretic ally founded on these same principles. The rights of free speech, free assemblage, and free press, are guaranteed to the people of this nation in its Constitution; but we have never had really free speech, nor a really free press, nor real freedom of assemblage; it has always been limited to 'freedom within the law,' which is not freedom at all. No country with the possible exception of Russia under the old regime, has so sternly silenced minorities

and otherwise denied its people these fundamental rights, as
the United States. Especially since the declaration of war, the
suppression has been so complete, so tyrannical, that thousands
of people who are most conservative, who would be horrified
at being called 'radicals' of any kind, are protesting against the
undue severity visited upon those who exercise their supposedly constitutional rights.

The immediate cause of my sending out these circulars was
the speech made by Elihu Root, in which he declared that
this is no time to think, argue, reason, or do anything but fight.
Mr. Root had put into concrete, concentrated form the motive
underlying all the emotional appeals made by bill boards,
music, the press, preparedness demonstrations, denunciation
of everybody who was anti-war as 'pro-German', 'Cowards',
'white rabbits', etc.,—all the hysterical jingoism which so often
goes by the name of patriotism, and which results in mob violence and such outrages as I shall show you have occurred in
this nation since the beginning of the war. Mr. Root's speech,
I repeat, was the immediate cause of my sending out these circulars. I should have infinitely preferred speaking face to face
with the men who had been called for war service. That, for
various reasons, was impracticable.

I had not money enough to hire a hall and advertise a meeting; I am not accustomed to speaking in halls; there was no
doubt in my mind that such a meeting would be prevented
or broken up by the police or military authorities; the mails
offered the most convenient method of communication available. The purpose was not to send these circulars to men actually in the service; the presumption being that such had given
the matter sufficient consideration to know what they were
doing. I fully expected that if any of the men who received circulars had enlisted or otherwise become actual members of the
service, they would understand that the communication was
not to them, but to drafted men, and disregard it. Not that

I considered these circulars improper reading for soldiers or sailors; merely that it was not my deliberate intention to send them to such.

The real issue in this case is, have citizens of these United States the right to confer together on the subject of war, and upon other closely related subjects? Have citizens who have been drafted, or who may be drafted, the right to think of their relation to the war and to the government, and of the relation of this government to other governments of the world, in any terms except those of complete acceptance of orders which may be issued to them by the Government? Are the laws of this country at the present time such as to demand for their obedience that citizens resign rights that we have been accustomed to consider fundamental in a democracy—namely, the rights of free speech, free press, and free assemblage? Has there been instituted in this country an autocracy comparable to Russia under the old regime, or Germany under the militaristic system which we officially protest we hate so much that we (officially) have entered the war to destroy it?

These are the questions you must decide before you can decide whether I have broken the laws of this country or not. If we are to take the words of President Wilson at their face value, it becomes at once apparent that the whole matter of the Conscientious Objector and his course of action is very simple, because, in his proclamation of May 18, explaining the Conscription Act, the President distinctly says that this is in no sense a conscription of the unwilling. Now the C. O. is decidedly unwilling to render military service; therefore, by the terms of the President's explanation of the act, he should be exempt from military service without further discussion of the matter.

But one who reads carefully must see that these words are not to be taken at their face value, because Mr. Wilson goes on to say that it is rather selection from a nation which has volunteered in mass. Now this nation has not volunteered in mass. This nation has not volunteered at all. If the nation had volunteered, it would never have been necessary to pass a conscription act.

From the beginning of the European war, this nation has been anti-war in sentiment. It has believed that the quarrel was a purely European one—a struggle for financial supremacy between England and Germany, in its essence—and it has had no wish to take sides, or to become embroiled in the war. President Wilson was elected on an anti-war platform. The slogan "He kept us out of war" was on every tongue—no, not every tongue. There were those who desired that this country enter the war, and they spoke bitterly against the peace program of Mr. Wilson. There were those who saw that, great as their profit was from munitions and war supplies sold to the allies, a still greater profit could be made if munitions and war supplies could be sold to our own government also; and it was from this source that the war agitation came. I have no wish to accuse the President unjustly. I do not know whether during all the time he was winning the confidence of this nation and promising to keep us out of war, he meant to plunge us in, or whether he simply has not been strong enough to resist the pressure brought to bear by the great financial interests of the country; but whatever the cause, the fact remains the same; an unwilling people have been betrayed into a war which they do not believe is a just one.

What should a nation do in such a case? To answer that, we must consider what a government is. What relation does it bear to the people? Such a government as ours, which we are in the habit of calling a democratic government, is, or should be, a means of expressing and carrying out the national will; that is, the will of the majority of the people who make up the nation. If it does not do that, it is not truly a democracy, but a despotism. As a simple matter of fact, whatever may have been true in the past, this government is not today a democracy. We have a machinery of government which on the surface looks representative; we have in fact that machinery so under the control of the financial powers that it is, as President Wilson has himself stated, no longer a government of the people, but of the interests. In his campaign speeches, portions of which have since been published under the title of *The New Freedom*, he points out, over and over again, the necessity this country is under, for the people to regain control of their government.

As means to this end, he urges that the people get together and discuss government matters among themselves, and make the result of their discussions known to the government. He says he would feel it a loss if he were deprived of intelligent criticism of the people. He says we must re organize our national economic life, even as we once re-organized our national political life; and that the way to do it is for the people to take counsel together and form an opinion as to what they want, and make that opinion known.

The Jails of this country today are full of people who have attempted to act upon President Wilson's advice. In this country, against whose 'peace and dignity' I am charged with offending, we have the preposterous spectacle which I will show to you:

Before war was declared, citizens were forbidden to hold peace demonstrations of any kind, such as peace parades; but preparedness parades, organized for the express purpose of working up war sentiment, were given encouragement and protection. Later, when the matter of conscription was under consideration, there were many arrests in various parts of the country of people who said publicly that conscription is an undemocratic measure, and urged the people to exert them selves to prevent its becoming a fact. We have had, here in Seattle, in the Wells-Sadler-et al case, an example of the treatment accorded people who exercised their rights of free speech, not even in criticism of an existing law, but in criticism of a thing which they saw was in danger of being forced upon this country as a law, and which they believed was contrary to the fundamental principles of our Constitution.

We have had the spectacle of a great representative body of the people, namely, the People's Council for Democracy and Terms of Peace, hustled about over the country from one city to another, from one state to another, its speakers arrested for inciting to riot and advocating violence, when in fact they had done neither the one nor the other; threatened in Hudson by a mob; in Fargo by the soldiers, though the Governor of Dakota wished to extend the Council his protection; in Chicago given such protection as the mayor could give, but compelled to disperse hastily in order to escape government suppression. Local meetings have fared no better. Scott Nearing, eminent economist, arrested before he had even a chance to speak in Duluth; in Oakland the Dist. Attorney organizing college youths to drown Mr. Nearing's speech in a flood of 'patriotic' songs! We have the spectacle of men being arrested for reading the Declaration of Independence upon the street corners; for circulating quotations from the Bible; for placing stickers upon enlistment posts; for a thousand trivial acts; for nothing at all.

Consider for a moment the labor situation in these United States during the past year. Forty corporations have made a net profit of $677,298,729 out of the war during the year 1916. That is not their total net profit; that is merely the amount by which their profit during the year 1916 is greater than their average profit during the three preceding years. Place opposite this fact the other fact that there have been serious strikes and other labor troubles in practically every great industry in the United States during the last year. When war was declared, there was a demand made by many corporations that all labor legislation be set aside during the period of the war, in order that women and children might be employed in occupations now closed to them, and also in order that employees might be worked an unlimited number of hours. There have been some voluntary advances in wages; but in no case has that advance been commensurate with the advanced cost of living. All attempts on the part of the workers them selves to obtain advances in wages, have been met with most bitter opposition on the part of employers. All attempts to secure better working conditions or shorter hours have also been bitterly opposed. The workers have been told that it was unpatriotic for them to desire more money or more leisure during war time. Nor has the opposition of employers con fined itself to peaceful, non-violent methods. We have had forcible deportations, as in Bisbee, Arizona, where some 1500 men, strikers and sympathizers and even some who might be classified as innocent bystanders, having no particular knowledge of or interest in the issue involved, were taken from their homes and left foodless, shelterless and comfortless in the desert. We have had, very close to home, and at an earlier period, an even more serious infraction of the laws and liberties of the people on the part of the employers; I mean the tragic incident of the 'Verona,' the ship on which at least five men were killed by officers who were proved to be absolutely under the control of the Lumbermen of the Northwest. We have had the Mooney case, in San Francisco, which is fundamentally a labor case, although the pretext upon which Mooney and his co-defendants were arrested was a bomb which exploded in the Preparedness parade—a crime terrible indeed, but utterly opposed to the character and purposes of the men arrested therefor. We have had the deliberate, cold-blooded murder of Frank Little in Butte, for his activities in connection with the copper strike. We have had the halls and offices of the IWW in all the principal cities of the U. S. raided, its property confiscated, its members jailed, often without any charge whatsoever being made against them. There are several instances of members being held 'for investigation' for as long as three months.

Men suspected of belonging to the organization have been arrested while going peaceably about their business over the country. Highly imaginative fables have been circulated to the effect that this organization had for its purpose this year the entire destruction of crops and other property. They have been accused of burning forests, in order to interfere with the production of war supplies. None of these charges has ever been substantiated, but the arrests go merrily on. The popular mind is still being poisoned against that organization by being told that it is a German spy institution; that it seeks to overthrow government and institute 'anarchy'; and the latest is that it is engaged in the illicit manufacture and sale of liquor and is a part of the great vice trust which is such a menace to the conscript army of the United States.

What has been the attitude of the government during all these troubles? Has it responded to the calls for investigation and relief from the reign of terror instituted by the employers and the 'patriots' who have wrought such a havoc among them? What has the government done? The murderers of the Everett victims walk free; so far as I know no investigation has been made of the Butte affair except the one made by Miss Rankin, and it has had no results; the Phelps-Dodge Company may continue to censor telegrams without fear of anything more serious than a reprimand from the government; government investigation of the Mooney case has had to be forced by protests from Russia; the government mediator in the shipyard strike adjusts wages so that they will be lower than before the strike, and gives the telephone girls so extremely small an increase in the beggarly wage they now receive that, here in Seattle at least, the offer is indignantly spurned. Consider that we have had also during the past summer certain race riots in which atrocities were perpetrated quite as horrible as any thing of which Germany has been guilty. Consider also that in this democratic country millions of women are denied so simple a democratic right as the ballot, and that women have been jailed and subjected to personal indignity and the bodily violence of forcible feeding for demanding the right to vote. Consider also that other women have been jailed and similarly treated for advocating that women should have the right of voluntary motherhood, and for teaching the women of the very poor how to lessen their misery and the misery of the children they already have, by limiting the size of their families. Consider that 17 men were recently lynched in Tulsa for no other crime than that they belonged to an unpopular labor organization. Consider that only the other day, in Montana, a secretary of this same organization was bastinadoed and two other members of the same organization hung by the neck until they lost consciousness. Other lynchings have been advocated as a necessary and patriotic measure. Con sider the outrageous treatment of the Rev. Mr. Biglow; the frenzied discharging of German College professors; the unutterable silly prejudice against every thing German. Consider these things, and then decide whether the condition of peace and dignity in these United States has been, or is, such that it can be offended or endangered by urging men to think of their duty to their country and their relation to a government which has so far shown itself unable, or unwilling, to safe guard its citizens against mob violence and other unlawful interference. The life of citizens in these States today is at the mercy of war-mad fanatics. We, who have boasted of being the land of the "free and the home of the brave, must, if we would preserve our lives and remain out of jail, seal our lips and lay our pens aside and submit to seeing our dearest and most cherished ideals of freedom and human dignity dragged through the blood and dust of war for the financial profit of those who keep us economically, mentally and spiritually enslaved. No, the United States Government today is not a means for expressing the will of the people of the nation. Yet, even in the face of these terrible facts, I have never counseled any man to forcibly resist the government in any way whatsoever. I have understood that such a condition as now obtains in the relations between this people and the Government of the United States, might breed violence. I have feared it, because I have believed, and now believe, that anything we as a people might gain by forcible overthrow of the existing government, would be less, and less enduring, than the results to be obtained by persistent, organized efforts to bring about the great economic and the social changes which naturally accompany economic changes, through means not involving violence.

I was opposed to military preparedness in this country for the reason that I understand that preparedness for war breeds war. If a nation learns to think in terms of war-preparedness, it is extremely unlikely that that nation will be able to see clearly that there are other ways of settling national difficulties than by wars. Furthermore, wars do not really settle anything. We are fond of saying that we gained our freedom from Great Britain by a war; but we are not, and have never been, quite free from Great Britain. Canada, which never went to war with the mother country, has been quite as independent as we; and today, as the ally of Great Britain, we certainly cannot claim freedom from her powerful influence. We also tell ourselves, and teach our children, that chattel slavery was abolished in this nation by means of a war. But the fact is that chattel slavery was becoming economically impossible in this country, and would have soon disappeared, war or no war. And even though we had gained perfect freedom from England, and even though we could have abolished chattel slavery only by a war, of what avail either of these accomplishments unless we, bettered the condition of the nation thereby? During the days of chattel slavery, one portion of the population was enslaved. Today practically the whole nation is in a condition of economic slavery, and, since the declaration of war, in a condition of military slavery as well. Plunged into war against our wills, we are compelled to support that war with every penny we spend, with every stroke of work we do, almost, I might say, with every breath we draw.

Our every attempt to free ourselves from this slavery is met with violence often of the most extreme character.

Gentlemen of the Jury, you have heard read a circular in which patriotic duty was analyzed, and the good of the country placed above obedience to its laws. This, says the prosecution, is treason, disloyalty, 'anarchy.' It is not treason to the best good of the people, whatever it may be to the established government. When the government deliberately, as in this case of declaring war upon Germany, violated the will of the nation; when there is no provision made for the people to make their opinion known officially—as, for instance, by a referendum vote—when the necessity is urgent for making that opinion known, lest irreparable damage be done, what course is left except for citizens to remain loyal to the principles of freedom and democracy for the perpetuation of which this nation is supposed to have been founded, even though it be at the expense of breaking a law in the making of which the people had no part? Is there anything sacred about law, just because it is law? Is there no place in this free country for those citizens who cannot act as the lawmakers would have them act, without violating their own consciences? Can it ever be to the best interest of any nation that its citizens should resign their freedom of conscience? I think not.

There are thousands, yes, millions, of citizens in this country whose conception of patriotism, of loyalty, immeasurably transcends mere obedience to law/ These citizens have come to realize the interdependence of all nations. No nation can exist unto itself alone. Just as the family conserves the interests of its members, just as the nation conserves, or should conserve, the interests of the States and communities of which the nation consists, so a world-state, a recognition on the part of all the peoples of all countries of common interest, is necessary to conserve the best interests of separate nations. Wars do not conduce to a furtherance or early realization of such a world-state. Industry today is international; art, music, culture, all phases of education, are international; the interests of the workers of all the world are identical, and the interests of all owners of industry, the financial powers, in all countries, is directly opposed to the interests of those workers. An early realization of a world state can be possible only when these facts are known and understood, and the old idea of national antagonism abandoned. Germany and England today are struggling for industrial supremacy. The workers of Germany and the workers of England will not be relatively much affected, no matter which country is victorious. The United States has entered the war on behalf of England, France, and the other allied powers, but the workers of the United States will not be much benefited by the war, no matter who may be victorious.

Wars tend to intensify national hatreds to a high degree. We hear much of this war as the last war—the war which will bring the people of the world together in love and amity. I have not much faith in the love and amity the German people and the French people and the English will have for each other when this war is over. It does not make us love our enemies to have those enemies murder our brothers and fathers, ravage our wives and sisters and daughters, and lay waste our homes. These things are being done on both sides. Germany has no doubt perpetrated atrocities; so has every nation that ever went to war. That is the nature of war. It is a horrible intoxication. In India, not so long ago, British soldiers tossed infants into the air and caught them on their bayonets. It is not that horrible people make war, but that war makes people horrible, that I find objectionable. I do not know how American soldiers may conduct themselves in this regard, but when I recall the atrocities perpetrated in these States, not upon battlefields, but in supposedly peaceful communities, I am not at all sure we shall not have some atrocities to answer for, equally with Germany.

I believe that the United States has thrown away the greatest opportunity to make the world safe for democracy that any nation has ever had. To America have come the peoples of all the earth; believing it to be a land of equal opportunity, where the freedom of which they had dreamed was an actuality. America has been aptly called the melting pot of the nations; a place where the various races were to be fused, and out of which was to come an understanding nation—a people unique in the history of the world, whose country should be, not like the old countries, a Fatherland, but a Brotherland—its people alone of all the peoples of the earth capable of understanding and loving all other nations, capable of using all that was good in the accomplishments and institutions of other nations, able and ready to lend aid whenever trouble arose between other nations; able because of its deep understanding, and ready because it would realize that only by safeguarding the rights and interests of each nation could the best good of all be secured. Practically unlimited resources, a clear field, untrammelled by tradition, immigrants in whom the love of liberty and the desire for a world-nation was strong—all these we had, and we have not used them wisely enough to avoid the horrible degradation and slavery into which we have fallen today.

Perhaps the most horrible thing about it all is that the great mass of citizens do not really know just where the trouble lies. They are well-meaning, they wish to be free, and wish others to be free; but they do not know who it is that has placed the chains upon us. Many of them do not even know that we are in chains. They have been so thoroughly taught reverence for constituted authority, and to believe whatever is told them by those in power, that they actually believe it is necessary, in order to be a loyal American citizen, to be the enemy of the rest of the world if ordered to do so by a few people whom we have allowed to gain control of the government. I am an American citizen, and I love this country. But I do not and cannot love it to the exclusion of other countries from my affections. To me England, which I never saw, but whose poets and scientists I

know and love and re cognize my indebtedness and the indebtedness of the world to, is as dear to me as Florida, which I
also never saw, but whose culture and whose scientific attain-
ments I also love and know myself indebted to. German music,
German science, German industrial efficiency, command my
admiration and respect, and those German people whom I have
known average neither better nor worse than those of other
nationalities. France, from which country my parents came,
has contributed her art, music, science, her gaiety, her splendid revolutionary spirit, to enrich my life and the lives of us
all. Russia—ah, Russia is today a glorious figure in the world,
advancing with proud and confident step toward the rising sun
of freedom, her voice lifted in the most wonderful song ever
heard during the ages. I love Russia as if she were my mother
country, yet I have never seen Russia, and have known but a
few of her people. I might continue thus, naming every country
of the globe; each has contributed something indispensable to
the life of our nation, and to the life of all the other nations.
And just as I love each of these countries, so I hate in each of
these countries the forces that keep them from attaining the
perfect state of freedom of which all peoples in all stages of
the world's history have dreamed. I hate the economic system
which decrees that millions shall toil for a bare living while the
few accumulate wealth and power which destroys them even
while they struggle still further to oppress the multitudes for
their own so-called benefit; I hate the stupidity of the masses,
which keeps them enslaved not only to their economic masters,
but to Custom, that cruelest and most ex acting tyrant of all—
that tyrant which blinds their eyes to the facts of their mental,
moral and spiritual slavery as well as to their economic slavery.
These things I hate, and against these things I must direct my
force and energy, such as it is, so long as I live. If to do this is
to be disloyal to America, then the greater must be preferred
above the less. I have no desire to maintain my citizenship in

these United States if to do so I must relinquish my citizenship in the Human Family.

Finally, it does not make an atom of difference whether you decide that I am innocent of any violation of the law or guilty of a crime. America will continue to be a country without dignity, without peace, and an offense to human kind, just as long as the present policy of tyrannical oppression and suppression is continued. So long as the people are denied the right to take counsel together, the right to make their wants and desires known to the governing bodies they elect, and the right to demand that those governing bodies act in accordance with the wants and desires of the people who elect them; so long as hysteria is our motive force rather than reason; so long as tyranny and force are used against the many for the aggrandizement of the few—just so long will America be a proper subject for scorn and abhorrence with all thinking people, unless their pity for its abjectness is so great that they cannot hate it.

And regardless of what your decision with regard to me may be, the principles for which I stand, the ideas which I have in a very limited way advocated, the work which I have tried to further, will be carried on, by more and more people, with a greater intensity and effectiveness; will those in power never learn that ideas can not be imprisoned? Will they never learn that, on the contrary, a vital idea only grows the faster when its suppression is attempted ? It has been argued that the tremendous force and vitality of the Russian Revolutionary Movement was due to the fact that all propaganda had to be carried on secretly. Russians have said to me recently, now begins to be some hope for a real revolutionary movement in this country. 'Now, when people are denied the right to think, now at last will they insist upon doing so.' I believe they are right in this prophecy. The people of America are awakening as never before. They have heard the first notes of the great hymn of freedom—and it is not a battle song. They are seeing clearly at last, that to be free means something more than the Revolutionary Fathers were even capable of imagining much less incorporating into the Constitution by which our liberties are supposed to be guaranteed to us today. They are seeing, these people of the United States, and the people of all the rest of the world are seeing it too, that there can be no equality, no liberty, no fraternity, so long as there is economic inequality, so long as any individual or group of individuals has the power to determine the terms upon which other individuals may live.

Political government is seen to be an empty shell, which has already lost its once-living tenant, political freedom. Industrial Government has moved into the empty tenement, and the iron hand of industrial power, of financial power, is our present ruling force. The only way in which the people can regain control of their government, the only way in which they can make the government democratic, is to gain owner ship and control of the industries. Our government will then continue to be an industrial government; but instead of being controlled by a small group of people for their own advantage, it will be the expression of the necessities and desires of the whole people. None of us can forecast exactly the final form of that industrial government; it is hardly possible that we shall choose to retain the cumbersome, expensive, inefficient machinery of political government which today serves only as a disguise for the actual governing body of the nation. But of this we may be sure: that government will serve the best interests of the whole nation, and that without prejudice to other nations.

There is a sense in which this is all aside from the question before you—namely, whether I did or did not advocate forcible resistance to the draft law, and whether in so doing I violated the postal laws. But I repeat that the real question at issue is not whether I did or did not advocate forcible resistance— the circulars show plainly that I did nothing of the kind—but whether it is unlawful to urge men to think on the most serious subject which can possibly affect their lives. With the contents of those circulars carefully borne in mind, and considering the fact that the prosecution has failed to prove any advocacy of force by me, it appears impossible to me that you should return any verdict except one of 'not guilty.' However, be that as it may, I have this further to say, and I am done:

The present war will settle nothing. The struggle for industrial supremacy will go on after this war in Europe is over; it will be settled by superior industrial efficiency, and industrial efficiency cannot be settled by force of arms. It must be settled by the application of intelligence to the needs and resources of the country, and by the conditions of the market. Ultimately, the highest degree of efficiency will be seen to be incompatible with production for profit.

Then production for profit will cease, and production for use take its place. Competition between nations will likewise cease. The greatest of all causes for war will be eliminated. The best brains of all nations will be set free by this termination of the economic struggle, for labors of science, art, and culture of all sorts. Then we may perhaps attain to a civilization of which mankind need not be ashamed.

These things will go on, whether I am in prison or out of it. They will go on, even though every Conscientious Objector, every pacifist, every I. W. W. and every member of any other union who endeavors to secure better conditions for the workers and freer atmosphere for thought and personal life, be thrown into jail. In a great world movement like this, the individual is of little importance; it is the propagation of the idea which is important. And all who are thus thrown into prison for the crime of loving humanity and working for its emancipation, will know that they are in good company; to them there will come the spirits and the memory of not only our own Revolutionary forefathers, and the Abolitionists, breakers of the laws of their times, but of all the great host of free-souled thinkers of all ages, from Jesus to Frank Little—revolutionists from England, France, Russia—there is no lack of good company for those whom we imprison today. And when they look out—if indeed they can see out of their prisons to where the 'free' citizens go their ways to and fro, they will not envy those outside knowing that a freedom of body which can be secured only by enslavement of the spirit is not worth having. Knowing, too, that every worker jailed means a quickening of the spirit in those outside, and increased de termination to redouble our efforts to bring about the reality of freedom of which the world has dreamed from the beginning, and which now, in spite of the horrible nightmare of war into which we are plunged, seems on the verge of realization.

Abbie Hoffman

**ABBIE HOFFMAN 1970**

ABBIE HOFFMAN WAS AN AMERICAN ANARCHIST and activist, prominent during the late 1960s and '70s. Hoffman and seven others were tried for conspiracy to cross state lines to incite a riot (an aspect of the Civil Rights Act of 1968), teaching how to make an incendiary device, and impeding police in their police duties, all in the aftermath of the police riot outside the 1968 Democratic Convention in Chicago, Illinois.

After Black Panther Bobby Seale had his case severed from the other seven defendants (following days of being bound and gagged in the courtroom), the trial became an incredible theater. Hoffman often appeared in court in costume, one day (along with codefendant Jerry Rubin) in judge's robes. When the judge ordered the robes removed, they revealed Chicago police uniforms underneath. Ultimately, all of the defendants were acquitted of conspiracy, but five (including Hoffman) were found guilty of the inciting a riot charge and sentenced to five years in prison.

Two years later, the US Court of Appeals overturned all of the convictions.

I feel like I have spent fifteen years watching John Daly shows about history. *You Are There.* It is sort of like taking LSD, which I recommend to you, Judge. I know a good dealer in Florida. I could fix you up.

Mr. Foran [the prosecutor—*ed.*] says that we are evil men, and I suppose that is sort of a compliment. He says that we are unpatriotic? I don't know, that has kind of a jingoistic ring. I suppose I am not patriotic.

But he says we are un-American. I don't feel un-American. I feel very American. I said it is not that the Yippies hate America. It is that they feel that the American Dream has been betrayed. That has been my attitude.

I know those guys on the wall. I know them better than you, I feel. I know Adams. I mean, I know all the Adams'. They grew up twenty miles from my home in Massachusetts. I played with Sam Adams on the Concord Bridge. I was there when Paul Revere rode right up on his motorcycle and said, "The pigs are coming, the pigs are coming. Right into Lexington." I was there. I know the Adams. Sam Adams was an evil man.

Thomas Jefferson. Thomas Jefferson called for a revolution every ten years. Thomas Jefferson had an agrarian reform program that made Mao [Zedong] look like a liberal. I know Thomas Jefferson.

Hamilton: Well, I didn't dig the Federalists. Maybe he deserved to have his brains blown out.

Washington? Washington grew pot. He called it hemp. It was called hemp then. He probably was a pot head.

Abraham Lincoln? There is another one. In 1861 Abraham Lincoln in his inaugural address said, and I quote "When the people shall grow weary of their constitutional right to amend the government, they shall exert their revolutionary right to dismember and overthrow that government." If Abraham Lincoln had given that speech in Lincoln Park, he would be on trial right here in this courtroom, because that is an inciteful speech. That is a speech intended to create a riot.

I don't even know what a riot is. I thought a riot was fun. Riot means you laugh, ha, ha. That is a riot. They call it a riot. I didn't want to be that serious. I was supposed to be funny. I tried to be, I mean, but it was sad last night. I am not made to be a martyr. I tried to sign up a few years, but I went down there. They ran out of nails. What was I going to do? So I ended up being funny.

It wasn't funny last night sitting in a prison cell, a 5' x 8' room, with no light in the room. I could have written a whole book last night. Nothing. No light in the room. Bedbugs all over. They bite. I haven't eaten in six days. I'm not on a hunger strike; you can call it that. It's just that the food stinks and I can't take it.

Well, we said it was like Alice in Wonderland coming in, now I feel like Alice in *1984*, because I have lived through the winter of injustice in this trial. And it's fitting that if you went to the South and fought for voter registration and got arrested and beaten eleven or twelve times on those dusty roads for no bread, it's only fitting that you be arrested and tried under the Civil Rights Act. That's the way it works.

Just want to say one more thing.

People—I guess that is what we are charged with—when they decide to go from one state of mind to another state of mind, when they decide to fly that route, I hope they go youth fare no matter what their age.

I will see you in Florida, Julie.

Bo Brown

**BO
BROWN
1978**

Rita "Bo" Brown was a member of the George Jackson Brigade, an American urban guerrilla group during the late 1970s based in Seattle, Washington. The George Jackson Brigade used expropriation of banks to fund it's militant activities, which included eighteen bombings of government and corporate targets over the course of two and a half years.

At her trial for bank robbery, Brown made two different statements to the court, a statement before sentencing, like all the others here, but also a closing statement to the court that was delivered before she was found guilty of robbing one bank (the feds declined to charge Brown with four other bank robberies that they believed she had committed) as a member of the George Jackson Brigade. She declined to plead innocent to the charge, instead using her closing statement to defend bank robbery, ahem, *expropriation*, as a tool of revolutionaries. Immediately after being convicted, but before sentencing, Brown was flown from Oregon to a federal prison in West Virginia, because of the state's (correct) fear of Brown being liberated by members of the George Jackson Brigade that were still free. Brown ultimately served eight years of a twenty-five year sentence.

*Court statement 1/11/78*

I am a member of a revolutionary organization known as the George Jackson Brigade. This group of freedom fighters has, and most certainly will continue to expropriate the funds necessary to promote guerrilla warfare in Amerikkka. This means that the GJB robs banks to help finance other revolutionary activities. This tactic is by no means new, or the result of any individual illness. This sickness is capitalism/imperialism spreading across the world destroying the earth and its peoples to satisfy its greed and need to own everything—the rich get richer and fewer.

The poor can continue to want more and have less—to pay 25% of their salaries to taxes, and the rest to barely survive—to live in fear of the state and its ever-growing police forces—to live in ghettos and prison cells—to live in fear of continual FBI illegal harassments, such as phone taps and sneak picture-taking, always in the name of intelligence, or they can get up off their knees and fight back!!! I have chosen to fight back, to resist, to work with others in doing what is necessary to see that our children have a future in which they will have control of their own lives. From each according to their ability—to each according to their need. This resistance, like everything else, requires capital. The banks hold this necessary capital and are vulnerable, so they become a target.

"Robbery" has been a worldwide strategy since the men/hunters invaded and enslaved the women and children of ancient agricultural tribes. This "robbery" literally ripped off millions of Africans, destroyed their cultures and made beasts of those who survived the slave ships. This "robbery" murdered and then confined the remains of Native American tribes rich with cultures of respect for all living things. This "robbery" has been the strategy of the very rich and very white ruling class, used to conquer and destroy. But this strategy has more recently reached a turning point. In the hands of the working peoples of this earth, this "robbery" is dead. A new concept, expropriation is born—to take rich private property for public use, to make the state pay for its own destruction. Today in Africa, in Asia, in Europe, in South America, and in North America, expropriation is a tool used to finance the inevitable revolution. Expropriation is only one of the many tools used to help expose and fight the real robber barons of the world.

A close study of the actions and communiqués of the GJB will clearly show that there is no desire or intention to harm any member of the working class. The immediate goals, as I see them, are to point out the crimes of the ruling pigs, to strike repeated solid blows to the belly of the beast (the oppressor state), and to encourage others to fight back by demonstrating that it is possible to do so.

The purpose of this room—all the big words used here, the games of slick dressing, the games of procedure, and the life and death power given to a few elite men is only another example of white, patriarchal ruling class intimidation. I consider this court to be a disgusting and sick mockery of justice. Guilt is commonly defined as feeling remorseful for having done something wrong. I feel no regret at having entered the US National Bank in Wilsonville, Oregon on February 7, 1977, handing the teller a note and leaving with $7,753. I do not consider it wrong to participate in the act of expropriating the real robbers/criminals. Nor do I consider it wrong for the people, felons or not, to possess a weapon. The people must be armed, and that is why I carried a firearm during the bank robbery.

Love and Rage—Fire and Smoke

*2/21/78 at sentencing*

I stand before this mockery of justice kourt to be condemned as its enemy—*and*—I am it enemy! I am a member of the George Jackson Brigade and I know the answer to Bertolt Brecht's "Which is the biggest crime, to rob a bank, or to found one?"

It is to my sisters and brothers of the working class that I am accountable, *not* to this kourt that harasses and searches my peers before they can enter what's supposed to be their courtroom, *not* to this or any kourt whose hidden purpose is to punish the poor and non-white in the name of the US government, a government which perpetuates the crimes of war and repression has no right to prescribe punishment for those who resist the continuation of worldwide death and misery. This government didn't ask its citizens what we thought about CIA intervention in Chile or US big business holdings in South Africa. I am a native fighting on her homeground. I was born and raised right here. All my life has been spent in Oregon and Washington. My parents are working people, my father a mill worker for 32 years; my mother an unskilled laborer at the county nursing home. We always had to count every penny and do without some thing or another to make it from payday to payday. I have pumped gas, been a clerk, a mechanic, a printer, and a variety of other things. That makes me a common working person, as is most of the population of this world. We have nothing to survive by except our labor—our sweat. We are slaves forced to give our labor and our lives to maintain an economic system designed to serve only the rich— almost always white male corporate owners. This ruling class has no respect for human life. Its only concerns are private property and personal power. They manipulate us as puppets on their stage of greed.

Right here in Oregon there are mountains of proof about how big business protected by the state and federal government rips us off daily. How much profit did Weyerhauser make last year? How much taxes did that company pay on those profits—if any? How come those who slave their lives away for George Weyerhauser get none of those profits? How come Weyerhauser can continue to pay small pollution fines and isn't made to install anti-pollutions systems? The answers to these kinds of questions will teach us just what George Weyerhauser really is and who he really cares about. Those cute commercials we see on TV are a snow job to keep us from seeing the truth.

There are few people in this state who know that the Wah Chang plant just north of Albany, right there on the freeway, is killing the pure air and water and even the earth so highly valued by Oregonians. For years we thought it was just a smelly pulp mill, but that was a lie! It is, in fact, the manufacturer of zirconium, a metal vital to the government's plan to pursue nuclear energy and warfare without properly considering the radioactive poison into our lives everyday! Their fines are minimal, they are not made seriously to clean up and say they shouldn't have to. The workers are in very real danger of serious illness or injury, and even death.

The University of Oregon has $3 million invested in stock in twenty-eight South African companies. The state board of education has passed the buck to the attorney general who has passed the buck to the state treasurer...the state of Oregon finances the most racist and genocidal government in the world.

The mountains of proof are everywhere!!!

Prisons are big business too. Nationally the annual profits reach $2 billion. Prisons promote "terrorism" by making the denial of human and democratic rights a respectable and common thing. Look at who is in prison and why—75% of all adults in AmeriKKKan prisons are Third World peoples. This is a clear and simple proof of systematic racism. Right now in Oregon there are three cruel and unusual punishment lawsuits—one at Oregon Correctional Institute, one at Oregon

State Penitentiary, and one at McLaren, the juvenile prison. Every person in this state should investigate these suits in their own interests. We all know it's the powerless working and poor people who go to jail. The real criminals, the rich—are pardoned by other rich criminals, or go to country club estates to do short time...(or—they can get "daddy" to put up $1.2 million for bail after conviction.

I am a womon who is greatly concerned that the biggest areas of neglect in this so-called justice system are rape, wife battering, and child abuse. The womon of today suffers every day from the oppression of sexism. Everywhere she looks she sees sexist stereotypes that scream—you are property—you are a sex object—you can't control your own body—men need to beat you sometimes—there is no such thing as rape—you must have asked for it. And, if she can't cope with this insanity, the male-dominated medical profession pronounces her crazy...90% of patients in mental hospitals are womyn.

I love children. To me, children are the most beautiful, honest, sincere, and creative human beings. It is for their futures as well as my own that I fight. My heart full of love for all people. My heart full of rage at the capitalist/imperialist system that traps and destroys us from birth. I am the anger of the people—like the thunder that comes before the rain that will heal the earth...

I am a lesbian—a womon who totally loves womyn. A womon who loves herself and her sisters. A womon who is proud to say that loving womyn is a very beautiful and positive aspect of my life. When any womon or man decides to be openly gay—to come out—we risk social disapproval, police harassment and the very real possibility of being beaten in the streets. We are denied jobs, thrown out of public places, refused housing, our children can be stolen from us, and most shrinks still think we suffer from some incurable sexual illness. This blatant discrimination is the systematic denial of our democratic and human rights. It should never be a crime for any person to love and care about another person. The freedom to be what we are is what we fight for! Womyn loving womyn and men loving men is nothing new. Since the beginning of time, we have loved free and proud. Our culture, though sparsely documented due to great efforts to suppress our herstory/history, does exist. During the time of Sappho and the Isle of Lesbos our sexuality was open and accepted. Then the self-appointed rulers—the profiteers—marched across the earth and for boots they wore suppression. Suppression to crush all who wouldn't conform to their ideas or recognize their right to destroy our various ways of life. We have been mighty warriors in many wars—Amazons and Roman soldiers. Not even Hitler—who killed us in one of his first experiments in annihilation—could destroy us. Joe McCarthy hunted us too. Today the fear of homosexuality is based in hysteria and ignorance. This kind of institutionalized fear is repeatedly used to keep us from building stronger resistance. It will work less and less as we learn to understand the tactics of psychological warfare used by the rich to keep us all in our places. But, we must remain alert to the very real threat of fascism and destroy it before we find ourselves surrounded.

It is necessary to define "armed struggle" and "terrorism," since these terms are often incorrectly used interchangeably. This error is continually made by the straight media who often just take orders from the FBI or other government gestapos. The press forget its real job is to report the facts to the people—not to use sensationalism merely to sell a particular channel or newspaper—and not to participate in news blackouts which keep facts from the people. "Terrorism" is armed action which deliberately and callously ignores the welfare of people. "Terrorism" is the institutionalized sick violence of the ruling class and its police forces, i.e. the senseless bombings of Vietnam; the Attica massacre; the Kent State massacre; the Jackson State massacre; the SLA [Symbionese Liberation Army] massacre; the individual murders of Clifford Glover,

Karen Silkwood, and George Jackson; the continuing murders and sterilization of Native Americans and Puerto Ricans; the inhumane method of confinement suffered by Assata Shakur (s/n Joanne Chesimard). "Armed struggle" is the use of controlled violence such as armed occupations, kidnappings, prisoner escapes, armed robbery, bombings, etc. A primary factor of "armed struggle" is that concern for the welfare of innocent people is always a vital factor of the planning and execution of these actions. Freedom fighters around the world have consistently made the distinction between revolutionary "armed struggle" against the ruling class and the "terrorism" of random violence used by the State against the people.

I am an anti-authoritarian lesbian feminist anarcho-communist. I am an urban guerrilla committed to give my white life if necessary! As our comrade brother George Jackson said—and it's just as true today as it was almost 10 years ago when he said it—"We must come together, understand the reality of our situation, understand that fascism is already here, that people are already dying who could be saved, that generations will die or live butchered half-lives if we fail to act."

Love and Rage—Fire and Smoke

**KUWASI BALAGOON 1983**

KUWASI BALAGOON WAS A BISEXUAL ANARCHIST member of the Harlem branch of the Black Panther Party, and the Black Liberation Army. Balagoon's politics became more anti-authoritarian as he became disillusioned with what he saw as authoritarian methods employed by the Oakland Black Panthers with regards to New York party leadership and priorities.

Balagoon's life was incredibly full of militant action. He was the only person convicted during a trial dubbed the "Panther 21," pleading guilty to attempting to kill New York cops. But by 1973 he had escaped from a New Jersey prison while there for an armed robbery charge, only to be recaptured 8 months later while attempting to free a comrade from police custody. Balagoon would escape from prison enough times to be dubbed "Maroon" by his comrades. In 1984 he was convicted of armed robbery and killing cops (and an armored truck guard) in two separate armored truck robberies. During that trial, he chose to go without a lawyer, refused to call himself a "defendant" (he preferred "prisoner of war"), and justified his acts to the court in four bold statements, the last of which is presented here.

Unfortunately, Balagoon's final escape would only come via death. In 1986 he died of pneumocystis pneumonia, an illness that at that time was commonly associated with AIDS. He was only 39 years old.

---

*Editor's note: Balagoon was part of a current that believed that capitalizing "We" and using the lowercase "i" pronoun were methods for decentering the individual for the sake of the collective. We maintain his spelling choice here.*

The ruling class of the United States and its government colonizes the New Afrikan people; that is, Black people held within the confines of the present borders of the U.S. i've been brought here to be sentenced by the state partly because all New Afrikans, notwithstanding a Black astronaut and Miss America, have been sen- tenced to an indefinite term of colonialization and partly because of my response to genocide, exploitation, oppression, degradation, and all the elements that make up this process of colonialization.

The bulk of New Afrikan people are restricted to living in certain areas, restricted to certain areas of employment; we, as well as other Third World peoples of color in the confines of the U.S., make up the caste of captive nations within this empire who perform the menial tasks far out of proportion to our numbers in relation to whites. Although the ruling class exploits all workers, they exploit New Afrikan and other Third World people at a higher rate. Our infant mortality rate is higher, our life expectancy shorter, our unemployment rates double, and none of this is by chance. This is contrived by the enemies of my people, our colonizers, the American imperialist, and this is enforced by force of arms.

Historically and universally the counter to imperialist armies are liberation armies, the counter to colonial wars are wars of liberation, the counter to reactionary violence, revolutionary violence. As a New Afrikan prisoner of war, i have no more respect for a sentence by the colonializers than i have for hypocritical legislative rituals leading to it or the enslavement apparatus of a corrupt order that commits genocide against entire peoples and threatens the entire biosphere or the pompous proclaimers of democracy and free enterprise in a country of racists, where less than 2 percent of the population own more than 30 percent of the wealth in a pyramid whose base is made up of 50 percent of the population earning less than 9 percent of the wealth.

The United States imperialist government colonializes New Afrikan people in every sense of the word, and every New Afrikan who investigates that fact and all that it means comes face to face with a dilemma: to deal with the condition on a personal basis and do the best they can under a circumstance that's dictated by what is in fact the enemy and leave the decision with others and perhaps to another generation, or to join with those of us commit- ted to overturning conditions for the entire New Afrikan nation and make war with those who historically and presently make war against us for however long it takes.

When the oppressed bear with it, accept colonialization for the most part, or at least don't get so upset about it as to entertain the idea of war, things are okay by pig logic. [District Attorney] Gribetz wishes out loud that there were a death penalty, but the fact that there has never been a white executed for the rape or murder of a Black in the entire history of the United States doesn't provoke any wishes for a need for change. Not one in all of the fifty states or colonies before them during four hundred years is an incredible statistic. But although he rants and raves, he doesn't challenge the truth of that statement or the recent murder of a Black man in Manhattan for writing graffiti on the subway or murder of a Black man in Boston or of the two in Chicago or a child in California, all by police; or the fourteen Black women murdered in Boston, twenty-five Black children murdered in Atlanta since the arrest of Wayne Williams, or the beating death of Willie Turks. These crimes don't call for the death penalty, if any penalty at all, all this is okay by pig logic: that kind of killing helps to keep the colonies in check.

When Somoza passed out the best land in Nicaragua to members of his family, sent his henchmen out to kill whoever disagreed and subjected the rest of the population to poverty, illiteracy, poor sanitation, and hunger and printed the face of an American ambassador on Nicaraguan money, everything was okay, there was no need to arm anyone to overthrow or "destabilize" that situation or bring a naval blockade to bear or talk about some other people's nation being America's backyard. But when the people of Nicaragua resolved to change their conditions for the better and remove all obstacles in their way, then it was time for "dirty tricks," a War Powers Act, and reactivation of the draft.

As long as the people of El Salvador suffered their best land given to the United Fruit Company (or whatever name it goes by now [It's now Chiquita Brand International —*ed.*]) and lived clearly under the heel of American imperialism, by pig logic everything was okay. But once people said enough and really contested it, well, it was time to fortify the puppet regime's army and send advisers, and when a Salvadoran patriot blew one of those advisers away, by pig logic it was a shame before God.

When the reactionaries killed journalists and nuns, it was cause for concern; when the reactionaries killed peasants and other colonial subjects, that was unfortunate, their names or even numbers were not noted. Just so many niggers. But when a career soldier, trained and armed to kill and direct intelligence for the purpose of more killings so that large corporations could continue to drink Salvadoran blood, gets killed, the culprit must be found right away.

When a cop gets killed, by pig logic it's different than when an old lady or a teenager or almost anyone else gets killed. Especially if that anyone else is nonwhite. When Mtayari Shabaka Sundiata was killed, they put a picture of his corpse on the front page of the *Daily News*, and then in the centerfold under the caption "Death to the Terrorist." They did this because he opposed the colonialization of New Afrikan people, and they make a big deal out of the deaths of the cops and money courier, because they impose colonialization and this is war.

Legal rituals have no effect on the historic process of armed struggle by oppressed nations. The war will continue and intensify, and as for me, i'd rather be in jail or in the grave than do anything other than fight the oppressor of my people. The New Afrikan Nation, as well as the Native American Nations, are colonialized within the present confines of the United States, as the Puerto Rican and Mexicano Nations are colonialized within, as well as outside, the present confines of the United States. We have a right to resist, to expropriate money and arms, to kill the enemy of our people, to bomb, and do whatever else aids us in winning, and we will win.

The foundation of the revolution must rest upon the bones of the oppressors.

AFTER BEING SENTENCED TO 75 YEARS TO LIFE IN PRISON, HE said "As to the 75 years in prison, I am not really worried, not only because I am in the habit of not completing sentences or waiting on parole, or any of that nonsense, but also because the State simply isn't going to last 75 or even 50 years."

Kuwasi Balagoon

**ANN HANSEN 1984** ANN HANSEN WAS A MEMBER OF THE CANADIAN anarchist group Direct Action, and later the Wimmin's Fire Brigade. In early 1982, Direct Action bombed a BC Hydro power station, completely destroying four transformers, resulting in $5 million in damages. Five months later, the group bombed a Litton Industries factory which was manufacturing guidance systems for American Tomahawk missiles. Despite warnings to evacuate the building, this bombing resulted in injuries to three cops, five employees of Litton, and three bystanders, in addition to the millions of dollars in damage to the Litton plant. The plant was out of production for about a week. Litton's President, without a trace of irony, said that "Bombing is madness." The Wimmin's Fire Brigade, bombed three locations of Red Hot Video, a chain of porn stores that was accused of selling snuff films.

Upon hearing her sentence to life in prison, Ann threw a tomato at the judge. Ultimately Ann was released from prison after serving eight years of that life sentence.

When I look back on the past year and a half, I realize that I have learned a lesson. Not the kind of lesson that some people would hope I had learned, but rather through direct life experience I have re-learned what I once only understood theoretically—that the courts have nothing to do with justice and prison is where they punish the victims of this society. For many years now I have understood that the justice system was actually a system of injustice when seen in the broader social context. I was aware that parliament is where men make laws to protect big business, wealthy individuals and the status quo. Police were employed to enforce the laws, courts were created to prosecute those who broke the law, and prisons were built to punish the guilty.

My faith in the justice system began to erode as I grew up and saw the big businesses ripping off people by selling poorly produced products at high prices, resource companies gouging and raping the earth, governments producing nuclear arsenals capable of destroying life on earth many times over, pornographic magazines that normalized and glamourized rape, incest and sexual assault, and Indians being herded into reservations to die. All these crimes against humanity and the earth are legal. They are protected and sanctioned by Parliament, the courts, the law and the police. This was all very wrong.

In Oakalla, where I have spent the past sixteen months, I have found that 70 percent of the prison population are Indian womyn, even though Indian people make up only one percent of the total outside population. This disproportionate number of Indian people in prison is reflected in prison populations across the country and reflects the racism of our society.

Everyone I have met in prison is poor. No one owns cars, homes, land, or anything. They are there because they were forced to commit crimes to survive in a society that has no place for them. They have never owned forest companies that rape whole mountains of their forests, or handled nuclear murder weapons or stolen oil from Arab lands to be sold at scalper's prices in North America.

In the beginning when I was first arrested, I was intimidated and surrounded by the courts and prison. This fear provided the basis for the belief that if I played the legal game, I would get acquitted or perhaps less time. This fear obscured my vision and fooled me into thinking that I could get a break from the justice system. But this past eight months in court has sharpened my perceptions and strengthened my political convictions to see that the legal game is rigged and political prisoners are dealt a marked deck.

From the beginning in January 1983, the police illegally orchestrated press conferences and furnished the mass media with evidence, photos, and information that became the basis for nationwide news stories convicting us as terrorists. We were portrayed as dangerous, psychotic criminals without politics.

Then our charges were separated into four separate indictments, of which the first was the Brink's conspiracy, so that we would be criminalized. This would make it harder for people to understand us as political people for our future trials.

During the *voir dire*, it became obvious through police testimony that the different police departments had committed illegal acts during their investigation. The Security Service in all probability watched the WFB (Wimmin's Fire Brigade) do the firebombings since Julie and I had been under intensive twenty-four-hour surveillance by the SS for days prior to and during the day of the firebombing.

CLEU (Co-ordinated Law Enforcement Unit) had committed illegal break-ins to plant the bugs in our house and in Doug's apartment among other illegal activities. But despite this, the judge permitted the wire-tap evidence. This taught me that there is one law for the people and none for the police.

But the event during the court proceedings that has had the most politicizing effect on me was Julie's sentencing. The judge ignored the fact that she had plea-bargained and slapped her with the maximum prison sentence suggested by the Crown—twenty years. During the sentencing, the judge said that this case is criminal not political, yet the twenty-year sentence contradicts this view and instead reflects the real political nature of these proceedings. The twenty-year sentence was justified by the judge as a necessary social deterrent, which indicates that the court is so threatened by the potential of social upheaval that it takes a twenty-year sentence to deter others. That is political. It seems that the severity of the prison sentence is in direct proportion to the perceived level of discontent in society.

I understand why I have participated in the legal system up to now, but, in retrospect, in order to be honest to my political principles, I should have refused to collaborate in this legal sham and instead simply stated my political reasons for doing what I did.

Since I didn't then, I have the opportunity to do so now. Over the last couple of days we have heard witnesses who are activists around the different issues. They have spoken at great length about their efforts and the efforts of other groups to prevent the testing of the Cruise and the construction of the Cheekeye-Dunsmuir line and to stop Red Hot Video. I think it has become fairly obvious through their testimony that in each case they had exhausted all the legitimate channels of social protest in order to stop these projects and businesses. It was because there was no legal way to stop these crimes against humanity and the earth that I felt I had to use illegal actions to do so.

I didn't just feel that I should; I felt I had a duty and responsibility to do everything in my power to stop these crimes. At this dangerous point in human history, we have a moral responsibility to stop the arms race, violent pornography, and the destruction of the earth. This moral responsibility far overrides any obligation to adhere to man-made laws.

I would prefer to live in peace but, when I looked around me, I couldn't find it anywhere. Everywhere I looked, the land was being destroyed, the Indians were victims of genocide. Third World peoples were oppressed and massacred, people lived in industrial wastelands, and womyn were being raped, and children molested. I could never live in peace, only quiet—the kind you find in cemeteries.

Even though I knew that a few militant direct actions would not make the revolution or stop these projects, I believed that it was necessary to begin the development of an underground resistance movement that was capable of sabotage and expropriations and could work free from police surveillance. The development of an effective resistance movement is not an overnight affair—it takes decades of evolution. It has to start somewhere in small numbers, and whether or not it grows, becomes effective and successful, will depend upon whether we make it happen.

I believe these direct actions of sabotage complement the legal radical movement and serve a purpose that it can't fulfill. Not that the legal movement is ineffective; although its efforts often fail to stop a project, its work will increase people's consciousness. The important thing is that the aboveground and underground support one another because our strength lies in unity and diversity.

Although I did do these three political actions, they were the result of the culmination of a legal struggle around the respective issues. In fact, the point of an underground resistance movement is to develop a strategic political analysis and actions that are based on an understanding of the economics and politics of the corporate state. Instead of reacting to every issue that pops up, we carried out actions that were based upon an analysis. This way, if an effective resistance movement does develop, we can be subjects who determine history instead of reacting to every singularly obvious symptom of the system's disease.

The politics of Direct Action saw the interconnectedness of militarism, sexism, environmental destruction and imperialism.

We saw that all these problems are rooted in the value system and way of thinking called capitalism and patriarchy. These values are passed on from one generation to the next through the institutions of this society—the multinational corporations, schools, mass media, church and commercial culture.

The main value of this society can be boiled down simply into one word—money. All life on this earth is reduced to its profit value by the capitalist economic system. Women, animals, Third World people, and the environment are reduced to a product and thus are objectified. Workers are valued for their productivity, women as sex objects, animals for food or furs, the environment for its potential as a natural resource base. If some living being is of no economic value in relation to the capitalist system then it is valueless. Consequently, traditional Indian people become victims of genocide and huge areas of the earth are designated as "Natural Sacrifice Areas." So the Litton action, Cheekeye-Dunsmuir action and WFB action, at least for me, were not issue-oriented actions but were our resistance politics transformed into action.

Contrary to the Crown's and police's theories, Direct Action and the WFB were two different groups. Of the five of us charged with the Red Hot Video fire-bombings, only Julie and I did the fire-bombings. There were no men involved with doing the fire-bombings. Doug, Brent and Gerry just happened to either live with Julie and me, or visit us. The WFB was not an ongoing underground group, it was simply a group of womyn who came together for the purpose of fire-bombing Red Hot Video because we felt there was no other way for us to stop the proliferation of violent pornography.

Direct Action carried out the Litton and Cheekeye-Dunsmuir actions. I do sincerely regret that people were injured in the Litton bombing. All precautions were taken to prevent these injuries and an explanation as to why it happened was released almost immediately after the bombing. But I must also add that I criticize the Litton action itself because it was wrong for Direct Action to place a bomb near a building that people were working in, regardless of the number of precautions taken to ensure that nobody got hurt. In carrying out actions, revolutionaries should never rely on the police or security guards to clear out buildings and save people's lives.

There is no excuse for these mistakes, and I will always live with the pain that I am responsible for, but these mistakes should never overshadow the incredible amount of pain and suffering that Litton contributes to every day and the potential for planetary extinction that the Cruise missile embodies. Every day millions of people are slowly starving to death because so much money and human effort is diverted into the international war industry instead of being used to feed the people of the world. In Canada, essential social services are cut so that the government can pour more money into the war industry and megaprojects. For example, the federal government has given Litton $26.4 million in subsidies to build the guidance system of the Cruise [missile].

The use of *1984* double-think has become an important part of today's psychological warfare against people developing radical consciousness. We experience it every day, even in this courtroom. I am called a terrorist—one who tries to impose their will through force and intimidation—by the court and press. But I am not a terrorist. I am a person who feels a moral obligation to do all that is humanly possible to prevent the destruction of the earth. Businesses such as Litton, BC Hydro, and Red Hot Video are the real terrorists. They are guilty of crimes against humanity and the earth, yet they are free to carry on their illegal activities while those who resist and those who are their victims remain in prison. How do we, who have no armies, weapons, power or money, stop these criminals before they destroy the earth?

I believe if there is any hope for the future, it lies in our struggle.

Bill Dunne

**BILL DUNNE 1984**

BILL DUNNE WAS ARRESTED IN 1979 FOLLOW-ing the successful liberation of a comrade from a Seattle jail. He was captured following a shootout with police. He was sentenced to 90 years on charges of auto theft and abetting an escape. In 1983 he attempted to escape from Lewisburg Federal Penitentiary, and received another 15 year sentence, which included 7.5 years in isolation at the notorious federal prison in Marion. It was at his escape trial that he delivered the following statement.

---

Through an apparent Freudian slip, your apparatus has lim-ited my adversary in this attempt to criminalize the non-crim-inal to the United States, and did not have the effrontery to abuse the name of "the people" by adding it thereto. You have demonstrated your utter disregard for those people by wast-ing mass dollars on this reprehensible charade to add some years to what already are functionally forever sentences. Your crime in this regard is aggravated by having been perpetrated in this time of economic privation for so many. How many old people have died of cold amid dog food cans for want of far less wealth than has been squandered on this opulent power game? How much has our future been mortgaged to malnutrition and ignorance as WIC food programs and education funds are cut, while government tries to show its omnipotence by expensively squishing a couple more of the powerless more than they can by squished? To what extent has the quality of life to come been sacrificed to the trappings and glorification of power and imperial government such as are represented by these proceedings. Only you and your brethren who are motors of this madness can answer. But the fact that you have gone through with this pointless demonstration of your purloined power tells me what that answer would be. Your stated intention to do so told me that acquiescing in my own oppression with a "deal" would not free the wealth you have misused to feed the people or otherwise serve their interests, and your subsequent actions confirmed that. Your practice says that it would much more likely be used for more tools of oppression, more chains, another bomb or bullet with which to kill someone struggling for freedom.

That practice also demonstrates your need to legitimize the illegitimate with form rather than content, and to try to fool all of the people all of the time. Toward that end, you have subjected me and my co-defendant, Ron Duarte, to this mockery of the idea of justice, and now intend to "sentence" me as you have done Ron, and so try to brand as criminal the legitimate exercise of the human rights to which any reasonable person would feel impelled when confronted with the conditions of imprisonment extant in the American Gulag Archipelago. But it is human nature to resist oppression, and though you may be able to cover that fact up with your power, and legalistic appearances, and slick public relations, you cannot change it. Neither can you legitimize with those forms the usurpation of the people's power by your small and narrow class of exploiters and oppressors. This will become apparent even to you as maintaining the ascendancy of that class necessitates increasing and more blatant abrogations of the rights you falsely call inalienable, and now sometimes grant for the sake of appearances. Even now, the credibility and legitimacy of your government gang, and the masters with which it colludes is being increasingly sabotaged as they assassinate their own character with their actions, of which this supposed trial was one.

Your collective hypocrisy and illegitimacy is manifest in, for instance, your violation of your own laws, Title 18, US Code, Sections 956-62 specifically, in addition to international and human law to export murder, destruction, and poverty in order to crush the hopes and aspiration of the Nicaraguan people. You do this by arranging economic and armed intervention to destroy the undeniably positive accomplishments they have made since overthrowing the hateful tyrant [Anastasio] Somoza, whose indisputable crimes against humanity you supported and encouraged. Under your hand, such reactionary terrorism is also heavily scattered elsewhere among the inhabitants of Latin America, sowing death and disaster for the benefit of only a small minority. You attempt to disguise its criminality with Red-baiting hysteria and vague assertions of American interests, by which you mean your ability to exploit the labor and resources of the people and profit from the wars of oppression for which you force American workers to pay. You cannot realistically claim legitimacy in the face of your perpetration of such crimes to steal the wealth and liberty of the people of that region.

That hypocrisy is also apparent in your violation of the Fort Laramie Treaty of 1868, amongst many, many others, between the United States and the Sioux Nation. Your laws meant, and still mean, nothing when it came time to steal land and resources and culture and even lives from the indigenous people of *that* area. And when they protested, they were murdered by shot, and starvation, and subterfuge. Nor has your gang made any moves to correct this genocidal oppression in the name of thinly disguised greed; instead, it moves to make its thefts complete and permanent with forced sterilization, discrimination, impoverished reservations, armed force, and efforts to turn sacred Native land into "national sacrifice areas." In the face of such crimes committed as a matter of right, any claim to legitimacy to say what is or is not crime, and impose punishment for it is laughable.

The hypocrisy and illegitimacy of your government gang's posturing as representatives of the people is further apparent in your support for British imperialism and its murder and mayhem in Ireland, even aside from direct participation in your own, in violation of international law, again, yours and not the people's. You are quick to brand as "terrorists" Irish Republican freedom fighters, but who are the real terrorists? Never has an Irish Republican killed a child with a plastic bullet, but the British occupation forces do it frequently, not to mention keeping a people divided and enforcing privation, desperation, and exploitation for the benefit of a relative few. And they do so without bringing *any* positive results, let alone those of the republican movement. You ostentatiously waste large quantities of the people's money, ceremoniously receiving such symbols and perpetrators of persecution and repression as the Queen of England and Margaret Thatcher, as well as other international government gangsters, but deny entry to, harass, and even jail people whose popular support is not predicated on torture and violence. In this manner, you sought to prevent, for example Sinn Fein elected representatives from explaining the plight of the Irish people to American ones.

And who are you to say who is a terrorist after your invasions of Grenada, Nicaragua, and Lebanon, and murder of their citizens on the basis of chimerical fantasies intended only to cover up your greed? Who, after occupying Puerto Rico in a manner very similar to Britain's colonial occupation of Ireland, and using over a quarter of its arable land in pursuit of military madness while its people are impoverished and hungry? The only real difference between the different imperialisms is a matter of degree, and so all you agents of western imperialism are forced to try to legitimize each other. But your unprincipled practices and the suffering you inflict in order to maintain your power and privilege make such attempts transparent and futile.

I could go on and on around the world cataloging the evidence of you illegitimacy and in such greater depth and detail, but that is not necessary as it is also obvious in your dealings with the people you purport to represent. By exploiting other peoples over the years, you have managed to secure control of enough of the world's wealth to attempt to buy off a portion of the North American population with somewhat higher living standards, and conceal your oligarchic tyranny, but that does not mean you have limited your exploitation and oppression to "over there." Your power and position is built in large part on the armed robbery and swindle of land and resources from Native Americans and the labor of slaves and droves of immigrants who were little, if any, better off than slaves. In grabbing it, there was no force or subterfuge to which your power elite and its government tools would not stoop to prevent the people from gaining meaningful control of their labor and lives, even if it did cost a little more exposure of your illegitimacy.

A.E. Vanderbilt's quotation "the public be damned" summarized the attitude of your class, and its actions demonstrated that attitude. What was the condoned mass murder of striking Pullman Railroad workers by Finkertons, if not a demonstration of your illegitimacy? What was the Ludlow, Colorado massacre of striking miners by National Guard but a demonstration that yours is a government of the few, by the few, and for the few? What was the racist internment of masses of Oriental people during the inter-imperialist war with Japan, but a demonstration that your only legitimacy is in your physical power to oppress? The demonstrations in the history of this country alone of your illegitimacy to make moral judgments, or any others, against people are legion, and beyond my meager ability to delineate. They are not, however, limited to the bygone past; the past only provides a showing of continuity to your pattern and practice of illegitimacy.

That pattern and practice continues in the present era as the corruption of capitalism and its chronic crises lead you to escalating repression in order to maintain the growth and authority of your class, despite that being at the expense of the majority of the people. You lonely (*sic*) lament the economic and attendant social hardships of which the people have been made victim, yet it is your class that engineered them. They enabled you to make massive demands on workers to surrender pay and benefits for which they had struggled for years. They allowed you to decrease the cost of labor by creating a large pool of unemployed and disorganized workers on the verge of poverty while increasing profits for those who, like you, produce nothing. Those hardships also permitted you to set up the conditions to insure that people would be pleased at having been squeezed out of their jobs by automation, runaway shops, commodity manipulations, and other devices, without having been made beneficiaries of the wealth they had produced, and which you use as the instrument of their dispossession.

Yes, the "recession" served the government and its masters well by making people content with less while they took more. It also made them think that an unemployment rate described by distorting statistical machinations as 8% represents good times, and helped hide from them all they had lost while the rich got richer. It also served to widen the gap between have and have not, controller and controlled, by destroying thousands of small producer/employers, either giving the corporate bourgeoisie greater control of goods and services, and so more ability to exploit, or depriving the people of those goods and services. On top of that, it also helped you divide the people in order to better rule them by forcing them to compete for increasingly scarce economic resources and encouraging racism, sexism, sectarianism, and other forms of divisive and destructive intolerance. That is why you created the recession. The evidence shows that it was not an evil that just fell from the sky, suiting bourgeois and proletarian alike.

How many people died as a result of this deliberate rip-off of yours? How many mothers lost children to an enhanced infant mortality rate, or had their lives locked into the limitations of poverty through malnutrition, exposure, substandard housing, and inadequate medical care. How many life spans were thus shortened? How many were murdered by your police, or semi-murdered with imprisonment for attempting to ameliorate their destitution illegally? How many people were made victims of a diminished quality of life by being subject to the vagaries of existence in a society that has been thus artificially deteriorated and impoverished? I know what your answers to these questions would be; your practice demonstrates them, and it does nothing to support the lie of you legitimacy.

In the face of all of this, your gang and its masters cry for "austerity" as the path to economic salvation, and to further plunder the people. There is not much direct profit in education and knowledge is power, and you do not want to surrender any of that, so you devote less and less of the wealth extorted from the people in the form of taxes to education. Housing and human services such as health care, nutritional assistance, day care, mass transit, and environmental protection are labor intensive and not so very profitable for you. In addition, forcing people to scrabble after these things and compete for them sows division and distrust among the populace, and insures that their time and energy will be used up on that instead of on seeing past your propaganda machine and organizing against you for better lives. Instead of providing for such social necessities, you squander the people's wealth at the rate of $250 billion this year on massive tools of repression, destruction, and death that have no socially redeeming functions, and create far fewer jobs per dollar than the services, facilities, and products so desperately needed by people now. Instead of making the people's wealth serve them, you pay bankers, and other elements of your class who do not produce, around $100 billion per year in "interest" on money "borrowed" to finance profits for the corporate bourgeoisie on socially unproductive items. Instead of providing real freedom and equality for all, you waste many further billions of dollars trying to create the appearance of liberty and equity with your repressive apparatus and show trials such as this. This is not the stuff of which legitimacy is made, and it is only your arrogance that leads you to claim that it is.

Neither is the fact of the double and multiple standards that you not only employ, but have codified in the laws you use to give further appearance that there may be some legitimacy to your hegemony over the present society. While victimless illegalities, acts of economic coercion, results of the ignorance you foster, products of your sick conditioning, political transgression of the status quo, and petty opportunism of limited victimization are subject to draconian pursuit, prosecution, and punishment, crimes that steal from, defraud, injure, and even kill, large numbers of people get by with marginal, if any, punishment, if they are detected at all.

Bribers, bribe takers, price fixers, inside traders, users of substandard materials, defrauders on government contracts, makers of dangerously inferior products, influence peddlers, waste producers, etc., etc., ad nauseum are subject to only comparatively minor penalties, and allowed to report at their convenience to "country club" prisons for token confinement, if they are prosecuted or incarcerated at all. Even a president who tried to steal the country, from you, for you have already stolen it from the people, got nothing worse than retired to a life of luxury. People struggling in defense of their lives, families, people, and human rights are much more likely to get forever sentences, or worse. The process by which you come to the imposition of such sentences shows that the "inalienable rights" supposedly inherent in it are little more than popular mythology dependent on the power to enforce them. How, for instance, can the same system that allowed the murderer of a San Francisco Mayor and city supervisor to raise the infamous "Twinkie defense," in which he alleged that a junk food diet made him crazy, and so not responsible, deny a person the right to explain the necessity for attempting to depart from the illegal, inhumane, immoral, and illegitimate conditions of the American Gulag, and still claim to accord equal protection under the laws? Not legitimately!

The fact that your law and government forms are merely a tool of control into which principle enters only marginally, if at all, is further demonstrated by the facility with which you shuck those elements thereof which run contrary to your perceived interests. You have whittled away at the First Amendment of your Bill of Rights to allow the suppression of publications such as Washington Prison News Service, and use its deprivation as a punishment in your prisons. The Second Amendment has been drastically curtailed, and is subject to increasing attack. The Fourth Amendment no longer allows for the security it was intended to protect, or did even as little as fifteen years ago. If this trial in which the right to a defense was denied is an example, the Fifth Amendment has been seriously damaged too. Likewise, this trial saw the contravention of five of the eight provisions of the Sixth Amendment. Your prison system, your gulag, puts the lie to the Eighth Amendment and your state and federal gangs have disenfranchised the people to the point that their inclusion in the Ninth and Tenth Amendments is meaningless. And the list goes on.

Should an element of your apparatus turn out to benefit the people to a degree displeasing to you, it is quickly moved against.

An example thereof in the US Civil Rights Commission, whose principled actions in defense of freedom were stopped and are now being rolled back. This was done through the base stacking of that commission with new and reactionary appointments that will vigorously pursue the interests of your class, as been demonstrated since the stacking. Similarly, the Environmental Protection Agency, through corruption and political manipulation, has been turned from a tool with which to safeguard and defend and insure the intelligent use of the earth and its inhabitants and resources, and irreplaceable natural heritage for the power and profit and greed of a few. Hence, we see that it is expediency and not legitimacy that is protected by your "rule of law."

Even the character of the repression you inflict on those to whom you have ascribed guilt of transgression of your laws shows your hypocrisy and illegitimacy to so misuse the people's name, authority, and money. In your present position of power, and in light of your current practice, I would not expect you to be particularly worried about one more exposure of the inhumanity you have created and perpetuate in the dark concrete corners of your prisons by a small and weak voice such as mine. Apparently, however, you are, as you took pains to insure that you would not be confronted with the conditions of the American Gulag during this trial. But the use of your physical power, the power of your armed henchpeople, to prevent those barbarous conditions from being brought out in support of our necessity defense does not mean they don't exist.

Still very real is the racism inherent in your ensignment of people to your prisons, and in the artificial divisions and conflicts you use it to create a means of control, regardless of the suffering and aggravation of existing social ills in which it results. Still very real is the brutality of prison officials and their quickness to resort to force and violence, their creation of circumstances to encourage violence between prisoners, and their maintenance of an atmosphere of tension, insecurity, and threat. Still very real is the increasing use of internal exile, the banishment of prisoners to distant prisons far from their families and communities, often in retaliation for the exercise of supposedly protected rights. And still very real are the murders, assaults, gassings, chainings for long periods, forever sentences, overcrowded and antiquated facilities, lack of opportunity for constructive pursuits such as education, recreation, and cultural activities, lack of any security in job, housing, property, or location, isolation from the community and the deprivation of any power with which to contest this victimization. All prisoners of your state are subject to these deplorable conditions, and all fall victim to their deleterious effects to some extent.

So, too, does the community you allege to serve suffer from those conditions. Despite the existence of far more productive means to deal with crime, you persist in maintaining the foregoing, and worse, conditions. Given your undeniable knowledge and vast resources, it becomes obvious that it is not protection of the community in which you are interested, but the creation of an anti-social force of damaged and deranged individuals who will prey upon the community and so give you an excuse to maintain your occupying army of police and repressive apparatus against and amongst the people.

In light of the foregoing sketch, it is apparent that you and your master's existence is predicated on a continuous series of infamous crimes strung together with a web of lies and deceit against anyone and everyone not on your side of the barricade. Once the thin velvet glove is stripped away, it can be seen that your claims to legitimacy are specious, and that to recognize such claims is to cooperate in your criminality. No reasonable person who has had the opportunity and information to see and analyze past the efforts of your propaganda machine, to see the iron fist lurking beneath the velvet glove, could do other than resist your illegitimate authority and its exploitation and oppression in one or more of the myriad ways available to we, the people. You can duck and dodge, lie and connive, but you can't hide; as your ability to disguise your illegitimacy decreases, more and more of your victims will see it and, when enough of them do, the people will rise, as my co-defendant, Ron Duarte, has already informed you.

Accordingly, I cannot, will not, and do not recognize your legitimacy to sentence, or do anything else to me, and feel you owe me an apology for having caused me to tolerate this farce, though I have no illusions at this point that you will act appropriately. To the extent that I have participated in the window dressing of these proceedings, my efforts have been an attempt at the resistance mentioned before. You denied me the right to present a defense to your accusations of crime, but I have attempted to use these proceedings to expose the contradictions inherent in them, and their lack of legitimacy, and that of what led to them.

Now, you will use the power you have stolen from the people to do what it is you are going to do, and pretend to justify the massive amount of money you have wasted in getting to this point. You will add something to the forever your gang has already imposed on me for political direct action in an attempt to make some arcane statement of your own. But I am not intimidated at the prospect, nor am I chastened by it, or moved to be obsequious before your power. All you can take from me is my life, and if you are going to do that, you're going to do it. A forever sentence plus 1 or 10 or 100 or whatever is still forever. You can enlarge the number, but it means the same and will not change what I know or think of will happen to me. So do now what you will, compound the crime. It means nothing to me.

**NIKOS MAZIOTIS 1999**

IN 1999, GREEK ANARCHIST NIKOS MAZIOTIS was tried for placing a bomb at the Ministry of Industry and Development in solidarity with the struggle of people in the Greek village of Strymonikos against the development of a gold mine. The bomb failed to go off, and police found a fingerprint belonging to Maziotis. Maziotis would serve 3.5 years of a 15 year sentence after being found guilty. Maziotis would go on to be arrested in 2010 for participating in attacks claimed by Revolutionary Struggle (RS) before disappearing while on supervised release in 2012. He was arrested once again in 2014, and is now serving a 50 year sentence for being a part of Revolutionary Struggle, a group that took credit for numerous bombings, bank robberies, and attacks on police.

---

First, I do not intend to pretend to be the "good guy" here, when I was forced to appear. I will not apologize for anything, because I do not consider myself a criminal. I am a revolutionary. I have nothing to repent. I am proud of what I have done.

The only thing I regret is the technical error that was made so that the bomb didn't explode, so that my fingerprint was found on it later, and I ended up here. This is the only thing I repent.

You must keep in mind that although you are judges, and sitting higher than me, many times the revolutionaries, and myself specifically, have judged you long before you judged me. We are in opposite camps, hostile camps.

The revolutionaries and *revolutionary* justice—because I don't believe that this court is justice, it's the word *justice* in quotation marks—often times judge their enemies more mercilessly, when they get the chance to impose justice. I will begin from many years ago. We don't have any crime of mine to judge here. On the contrary, we will talk about crimes, but not mine. We will talk about the crimes of the State, of its mechanisms, of justice, and police crimes...

The biggest lie of all time is that the State is society. I think Nietzsche also said that the State lies. We are opposed to the division of society into classes, we are against a separation between those who give orders and others who obey orders. This authoritarian structure penetrates the whole of society and it is this structure that we want to destroy. Either with peaceful, or with violent means, even with guns. I have no problem with that.

I will contradict my brother who said before, that he didn't want the guns in order to make war. They were for war. Maybe they were just kept there [at his home]. But guns are for war, you don't just have them to keep them at home. I might have kept them as they were, but they are to make war and I make war...the bomb in the Ministry was an act of war.

Our purpose, within the anti-State and anti-capitalist struggle, is to connect ourselves with other social struggles. Our purpose when intervening in these struggles is also to attempt to make things reach the edge, which means to culminate with the conflict of these social struggles with the State and the police. To urge the people fighting to go beyond institutional models, the trade unions, the local administrations, and all these manipulators who are enemies of human freedom. Many comrades of mine, with their small forces, were engaged in such struggles. I will tell you about them more specifically. In 1989, in a struggle of environmental interest in the village of Aravissos, the residents of the area didn't want their water sources to be exploited by the water company of Thessaloniki. They clashed with the police and the riot police, they burned water pumps, they set fires, and put up barricades. And some of our comrades from Thessaloniki took part in this struggle and they were even arrested...

Generally, wherever there are disturbances, there are conflicts we want to be in. To subvert things. For us, this is not a crime. In a real sense, these disturbances are the "popular sovereignty" that professional politicians keep talking about. That's where freedom is expressed...

Now let's talk about the struggle of the people in Strymonikos. Long before I placed the bomb, other comrades had been to the villages, they had been talking with the people there, they had published a pamphlet about this revolt, about the clashes in October of 1996. But I will talk more specifically about the struggle in Strymonikos in a little while. First, I want to talk exclusively about the action.

To tell the truth, I was inspired to place this bomb for a specific reason: the people of the villages had surpassed the limits, by themselves. If it was a struggle inside an institutional framework, in the way that trade unions and local administrations try to keep these struggles restricted, if it was confined in a mild, tame, and unthreatening protest, maybe I wouldn't have done anything.

But the comrades up there in the villages—who are not anarchists of course, but I don't care about that, they are citizens who also want their freedom—had surpassed every limit.

They had conflicts with the police three times—on the 17th of October 1996, on the 25th of July '97, and on November 9th '98—they had set fire to police cars and riot police vans, they had burnt machinery belonging to TVX [a Canadian gold mining company—*ed*.], they had invaded the mines of Olympiada and destroyed part of the installations. Some of them also became a sort of guerrilla. During the night, they were going out with guns, shooting in the air to frighten the policemen. And I thought, these people are cool, they've gone even further than us. And then repression followed, especially in '97 when martial law was imposed in the area.

The Chief of Police in Halkidiki gave an order according to which all gatherings and demonstrations were forbidden. They also sent special police units and police tanks, which appeared in the streets for the first time since 1980. And now they were sending them out again, in the villages of Halkidiki. So, I thought, we must do something here, in Athens. It is not possible that others are under repression and we here stay passive.

The Ministry of Industry and Development, on Papadiamadopoulou and Michalakopoulou Streets, was one of the centers of this case. The struggle in Strymonikos was a struggle against "development," against "modernization" and all this crap they keep saying. What is hidden behind all these terms is the profits of multinationals, the profits of "our own" capitalists, Greek capitalists, the profits of state officials, of the Greek state, of the bureaucrats, of all those who take the money that comes in, of tech companies...there is no relation between this "development" and "modernization" they are talking about, and the fulfillment of popular needs. No relation at all. So, I placed a bomb.

The purpose was the one I said in the letter with which I took responsibility for the action. In the passage of February 1998 I said in placing the explosive device my purpose was to send a double political message. Everything is political. Even if you use such means, the messages are political. War itself is a means of political pressure. In this case, this was also a political means, a political practice.

First of all, it was a message to the people of Strymonikos that "you are not alone, there are also others who may live 600 km away from you, but they care." Not for personal reasons...I don't know anyone from there personally. Other comrades know people from there. I haven't even been there. It was not my house that was threatened, but this is not the point.

Simply, my principle, and generally the principle of the anarchists and of other non-anarchist revolutionaries is that social freedom is one and inseparable. So, if freedom is partially offended, in essence it is offended as a whole. If their freedom is offended, mine is offended too. Their war will be my war, especially in an area where the "sovereign people"—again an expression used by professional politicians—does not want what the State and Capital want: the gold mine of TVX.

On the other hand, I have said that, okay, there would be some damage—I knew that. Yes, I had the intention to cause material damage. So, what damage would that be? On the windows, in that specific place, what kind of damage? Or outside the storehouse where I placed the bomb? According to me, the damages would be minimal. But even if they were more than minimal, for me it is not important at all. Because freedom can't be compared with the material damages of some windows, of a state car or state-property. For me, the Ministry is not an institution of common benefit as the charges say. Of state benefit, yes, but not of any social benefit. However, even if the device did not explode, I sent my message...

I will refer a little to the technical aspects. Exactly because I am a social revolutionary—and when you say that, it is like talking about what is for the benefit of society. Not "like." It *is* for the social benefit. As I have this principle, I couldn't harm any citizen. I could harm a policeman. I consider them my enemies. And you are my enemies too. I distinguish you. I make a clear class separation. On one hand we have those, on the other hand, we have the others. On this occasion though I didn't intend to harm either the policeman who guarded the Ministry, or anybody else; and of course not a citizen.

The procedure that is used by groups or individuals, in general, is exactly this: you first place the bomb at your target and then you call a newspaper. In that case, I called to *Eleftherotypia* and said: In half an hour a bomb will explode there. Exactly what is written in the evidence: In 30 minutes there will be an explosion in the Ministry of Industry and Development, because of the case of TVX in Strymonikos. Whether the bomb exploded or not there was absolutely no danger to human lives. In the case that it exploded, there would be only material damages. So, it would happen exactly as I intended. Objectively, if the device had exploded there was no chance of an accident, such as exploding before or after the time given...

I want to refer more to what I call solidarity, to the motives that I had. What is this solidarity? I believe...that human society was created, based on three components: solidarity, mutual aid, and helping each other. So, that's what human freedom is based on. Any social group in struggle, in a different place and time, whether they are pupils, or farmers, or citizens of local societies, for me and for the anarchists these struggles are very important. It doesn't have to do with whether I am a worker and identifying my interests with the interests of that class. If someone asks for a higher salary or has a trade unionist demand, for me it is not important. For me, solidarity means the unreserved acceptance and support with every means of the right that the people must have to determine their lives as they wish, not letting others decide in their place, like the State and Capital do.

That means that in this specific case, of the struggle of Strymonikos but also in every social struggle, for me what counts the most is that they are struggles through which the people want to determine their fate alone. And not having any police chief or state official or capitalist deciding what they should do. It is of secondary importance if they want or don't want the factory, if the focal point of the struggle is environmental. The important thing is that they don't want the factory because they don't like something imposed on them with violence.

Concerning the matter of political violence now...from the very beginning, they tried to present a case about "repulsive criminals" and "terrorists" who "placed 'blind' bombs": something that doesn't exist. If, theoretically, terrorism is exercising violence against citizens and an unarmed population, that definition applies exclusively to the State. Only the State attacks civilians, that's what the mechanisms of repression are for: the riot police, special repression police units, the army, special forces...mechanisms that also rob the people. They finance armed professionals, policemen. Aren't they trained to shoot real targets? Aren't the riot police armed with chemical gas? To use them where? On citizens, in demonstrations. So, only the State exercises violence against the citizens. I didn't use any violence against any citizen. I will say exactly what terrorism is.

Terrorism is when occupations, demonstrations and strikes are being attacked. When the riot police attacked the pensioners who demonstrated outside Maximou four years ago...

Terrorism is when special police forces invade the Chemistry School and beat up anarchists and youth...

Terrorism is when citizens are murdered by the police in simple "identification controls"...

Terrorism is when Ali Yumfraz, a Pomak from Vrilisia suburb of Athens, was arrested for being drunk and later was found dead in his cell in the police station...

Terrorism is this court, here. Every trial of a militant, every trial of a revolutionary is terrorism, a message of intimidation for society. I said it again in my statements yesterday, when you called me to ask if I accept the charges, and I will repeat it. Because of my persecution being political, the message is clear: whoever fights against the State and Capital will be penalized, criminalized and given the characterization of terrorist. The same for any solidarity with any social struggle: it will be penalized and put down. This is the message of this trial and by this sense it is terrorism. Terrorism against me, terrorism against the anarchists, terrorism against the people of Strymonikos, who are also receiving similar messages right now, as they have similar trials for their mobilizations. This is terrorism. The fact that I planted a bomb as an action of solidarity is not terrorism. Because no citizen was harmed by this action.

What the state wants is to deal with everyone alone. You must have heard an expression that Prime Minister Simitis is using a lot, talking about "social automatism" whenever social reactions burst out. He uses this expression in order to present these social reactions—the blockades in the streets, the squatting of public buildings and all the actions of this kind—as being in contrast with the interests of the rest of society... something that is a total lie. It is just the tactics of "divide and rule," which means "spread discord to break solidarity." Because solidarity is very important, as anyone who is alone becomes an easy target. When a workers' strike takes place and there is no solidarity, it is easier for it to be attacked. They talk about a "minority." This is the argument of the state, that it is "a trade unionist minority having retrogressive interests which turn against modernization, against development, against all the reforms" and all that nonsense. Well, there hasn't been one social current or social group that didn't come up in conflict with the State, especially during the 1990s, and that hasn't been faced with the argument that "you are just a minority," that "your struggle is in contrast with the rest of society's interests." That is exactly what happened in all cases...the same thing happened of course with the people of Strymonikos.

What is really being attacked is solidarity. And that's what is also attacked, without any disguise, through my trial. The State wants to attack everyone individually. Because when it finds them together, things are much more difficult.

Finally, I am not on trial because I placed a bomb, nor because I possessed three guns and ten kilograms of dynamite. After all, the army and the police have a lot more guns than me, and they use them. The one can't be compared with the other.

I have nothing else to say. The only thing I'll say more is that no matter what sentence I am convicted with, because it is certain that I will be convicted, I am not going to repent for anything. I will remain who I am. I can also say that prison is always a school for a revolutionary. His ideas and the endurance of his soul are experienced. And if he surpasses this test he becomes stronger and believes more in those things for which he was brought to prison. I have nothing more to say.

I want to complete what I was telling the public prosecutor before, about terrorism on an international level. In reality, at this moment, the US is the global police and terrorist, as the only great world power left. Which means it is the worst thing on Earth. And according to our perception—as anarchists—the State, all the states and all the governments are antisocial, terrorist mechanisms, since they have organized armies, police, hired torturers. I also want to complete what I was saying about having two weights and two measures. For example, the US provides weapons and finances, and instigates every dictatorial regime all over the world, in Greece as well. In Latin America, Chile, Argentina, Bolivia, Peru...this is Terrorism. Terrorism is to arm dictators, to arm death squads in Argentina, or in Bolivia in order to kill people of the Left, citizens, revolutionaries. Those who equip the death squads to torture, those are the terrorists. Terrorism is when they bombard Yugoslavia for ten days, killing civilians.

Excuse me, Mr. Prosecutor, but the US are the ones who say who is a terrorist and who isn't. Their State Department issues official directions, advising Greece about who is a terrorist. At this time, they place pressure on the Greek state to make an anti-terrorist law, a model of law which will criminalize those who fight, to make laws which are more draconian than those already existing...these are Terrorism.

The revolutionaries and the militants are not terrorists. The terrorists are the states themselves. And with this accusation, with this stigma, all states and governments try to criminalize the social revolutionaries and the militants inside their countries. The internal social enemy...however, I consider the State, justice, and the police to be this kind of enemy. As an internal social enemy. On the basis of the division I described before. That's the way the State sees it. This is what is set forth in this trial.

Public prosecutor: *What do you have to oppose to the existent?*

Social revolution. By any means necessary. It is generally proven, because I am well versed in Greek, as well as in international social and political history, that no changes have ever come about, never did humanity achieve any progress—progress as I conceive it—through begging, praying, or by means of words alone.

In the text I sent to claim the action, when I said that I placed the bomb, which was published in *Eleftherotypia* newspaper, I said that the social elite, the mandarins of capital, the bureaucrats, all these useless and parasitic people—that should disappear from the proscenium of history—they will never give up their privileges through a civilized discussion, through persuasion. I don't want to have a discussion because you can't have a discussion with that kind of people...

I would like to add something. Exactly because I have studied a lot, (I know that) during the events of July of '65, a conservative congressman of the National Radical Union came out and said about those who went down to the streets and caused disturbances, when Petroulas was killed, that "democracy is not the red tramps but we, the participants in the parliament," which means the congressmen who are well paid.

I will reverse that. Popular sovereignty, honorable judges, is when Molotov cocktails and stones are thrown at the police, when state cars, banks, shopping centers and luxury stores are burnt down...this is how the people react. History itself has proven that this is the way people react. This is popular sovereignty. When Maziotis goes and places a bomb in the Ministry of Industry and Development, in solidarity with the struggle of the people in Strymonikos. This is the real popular sovereignty and not what the Constitution says...

Pola Roupa

Nikos Maziotis

**POLA ROUPA 2011**

Pola Roupa is a greek anarchist, a member of the urban guerrilla group Revolutionary Struggle. For more than a decade, RS attacked symbols and institutions of the State and Capital. Roupa, along with her partner Nikos Maziotis, and four others, was arrested in 2010, and charged with membership in the group. But due to a Greek law that states that one must be released from jail after 18 months without conviction, Roupa and Maziotis were able to go underground. Maziotis was rearrested in 2014. In February 2016, Ropa attempted to use a helicopter to liberate Maziotis from prison, but the helicopter pilot resisted. Ropa escaped from the scene. Following this attempt, a one million euro bounty was put on her head. She was ultimately captured in 2017 and sentenced to 50 years in prison, not for any specific acts, but for belonging to Revolutionary Struggle. The following statement was given to the court prior to her 2011 release that facilitated the escape.

Let me begin by commenting on the main accusation against us, that we have founded a "terrorist organization," by which "we were targeting the country's established constitutional order, seeking its overthrow or even its alteration." I would like to underline this point. This charge by itself is the biggest proof that this is in fact a political trial. There is no better confession that this is an armed group which has turned against the establishment, against the established order. This charge by itself is a confession that we are political subjects, who have shared political objectives, and that the action of our group was clearly political.

However, you do not admit that we are a political organization, because this would in fact be an indirect admission that there is some political rival to this system; namely that Revolutionary Struggle is a political organization which advocates another type of society; another type of social, political and economic organization. An acknowledgment of the fact that you are facing political adversaries would actually mean you acknowledge that within this society, this system you loyally serve, there are people who are struggling, looking, standing, striving for another type of social organization.

This alone would be a blow to the very same establishment you serve. On the other hand, however, you wish to present this establishment as a monolith; namely that there is no life outside this system; that there is no life outside this society. You would like to convince everyone that any attempt, any struggle to liberate ourselves from this social situation would be disastrous. You would like to convince everyone that the existence of a stateless-society, without managers and subordinates, is impossible. You would like to convince everyone that the existence of a society without masters and slaves is impossible. You would like to convince everyone that the existence of a society without rich and poor is impossible. Obviously this line of thinking has a political and theoretical background. We know that much. There are theorists such as Thomas Malthus and Adam Smith, and there have been many throughout the history of the capitalist system you serve, who theorized the existence of poverty, who theorized the notion that the existence of a society beyond social divisions is impossible.

This is something you yourselves also serve through this court proceeding; this entire theory, which in reality seeks to convince people that the fate of the poor is to be poor, the fate of the oppressed is to be oppressed, and as Smith said—and those who are familiar with his papers know that—the pursuit of profit, the very concept on which a society of inequalities and injustices as ours is in fact based, is the inalienable right of everyone to improve their financial status by walking on other people's heads. This is what you consider to be everyone's inalienable right. To you, this could be characterized as "economic freedom." It's what you defend—the mere effort to legitimize the establishment's criminal nature. It's exactly this establishment we have tried to overthrow as an organization. This society of inequality is what we wish to overthrow.

I would now like to refer to an example in relation to a ruling of the Supreme Court concerning its response to an appeal against the court decision in the case of the Revolutionary Organization 17 November (17N). In response to an issue also examined by your court, namely the question of *"terrorist"* organization and political *"crime"*—words should be in quotation marks as terms used by the judiciary and not myself—the Supreme Court cited the objective theory arguing that, when someone turns to action against the country's established constitutional order and seeks its overthrow or even its alteration, in order for this action to be classified as political, the intent alone does not suffice—even if you all may acknowledge political motives as for the intent—but rather the outcome of this effort determines whether or not the action is political. In other words, the Supreme Court ruled that a judgment on the issue should depend on the result, so if we have failed to really over-throw the establishment, we are not deemed political prison-ers, and our case does not have a political nature. This is yet another confession. What kind of confession? The judiciary admits, "We go with the winner." In other words, the Supreme Court said, "If you had managed to win, then you would have been recognized as political beings. Since you didn't manage to do that, your action is not political. You hold a minority activity."

It is only logical that an organization such as Revolutionary Struggle cannot overturn the system alone. It takes entire polit-ical and social processes for this to succeed. But if we assume that Revolutionary Struggle did manage to overthrow the establishment, what would that mean? It would mean that we would automatically be recognized as political subjects. We would cease to be *terrorists* because we would be *winners*. What does this point to? That this court, just as the entire culture prevailing in this system says, "We go with the one who wins." This actually means, "We are not interested in the quality of this system. We are not interested in the quality of this organization. What interests us is who is on top." It is the winner who defines who is a political prisoner, which is a polit-ical trial, who is the political subject, and who is the criminal, who is a terrorist, and who is the one that can be vilified as a criminal offender.

I take it for granted that in a society like ours, as it exists today, in a society dominated by the State as a mechanism of Power, it is inevitable that the values of this society will be defined by whoever wins; by whoever has power in their hands. That is who will give meaning to things. Whoever struggles from below will be determined by those who dominate in terms that they choose.

This is the case here, too. The reality is that you yourselves would have to immediately change your attitude and recognize "political subjects" in any one group that managed to overturn the existing order.

Similarly, let's suppose that there had been a social revolution, and we had managed to overthrow this establishment, this very system. If this was the case, we can easily imagine the prime minister (Papandreou, for example) attempting to combat this revolution; to organize, bring troops in and put an end to our social attempt to subvert the established order. In this case, according to your line of argumentation, since it would be the prime minister who would be defeated, he would also be a terrorist, he would be a criminal. After being defeated, there's no way he could be a political subject any longer. Of course, this is only for the sake of argument, because if we were the winners there would be no question of accusations.

Now I would like to take a position on issues raised also by comrade Maziotis that concern who can speak of terrorists, from which position they speak, and whom they accuse of being terrorists.

In reality—as we mentioned in our [statement] on the first day of this trial—Revolutionary Struggle is clearly a political organization that has deep social and class characteristics, fighting for economic equality and political freedom for all people.

It is truly outrageous, especially under the conditions we live in today, that we are accused of being terrorists, when all that is happening around us constitutes a huge crime.

What this court serves is an economic and political system in deep crisis; a crisis that is the result of a long process of profound oppression and exploitation across the globe, the impacts of which are experienced today by all people. The "honorable gentlemen" of the system, investors, industrialists, capitalists, are in reality indifferent to people's lives, and in fact, profit is the only value to them. They go and invest in stock markets, which are nothing but a temple of money and a mechanism that legitimizes the euthanasia of entire parts of the population worldwide. As an organization, we went and blew up the stock exchange building, and we admitted we did so, and we did well—I bring the example of an action for which you accuse us based on your criminal law. Every "reputable" capitalist goes to the stock market with his Samsonite bag, and tie round his neck in order to increase his own profit and his own property, investing in human lives as if they were peanuts. It makes no difference to that capitalist if he's investing in peanuts, in indebted countries, or in people's death. Anyone who has elementarily dealt with these issues (because one does not need to have a degree in Business from some economic faculty to learn these things), anyone who has addressed at an elementary level what it means in our time to invest in stock markets, in food stock markets, in derivatives exchanges that the big-time investors themselves classify as weapons of mass destruction, must realize that indeed such investments result in the deaths of literally hundreds of thousands of people.

Recall the recent global food crisis, in 2008, which pushed millions of people to the streets. Many people died. Many more were marginalized. Entire classes of people were rendered extinct, thrown out of the picture.

The elites preach that the remedy for this crisis we are experiencing today is this social euthanasia, as I call it, which is presented as the only way to actually save the system from decay and to give it a breath of life. They are prepared to put people to death, not only to marginalize others but to kill people in cold blood, in order to survive. I will further analyze this in my final statement to the court. It's a long story and analysis that I believe Revolutionary Struggle has already offered and will be revived in this courtroom as well.

I believe it is utterly ridiculous that this system should accuse us of being "terrorists," when we are fighters, and have been since our teens, when most of us have been arrested and in many cases been beaten by cops, when we've been dragged into court many times because of protests, squats, or occupations and demonstrations, when we've acted in so many ways for a common struggle in the streets, when we've fought in the context of Revolutionary Struggle that, I repeat, is a political organization with profound social and class characteristics, when we've factually stood in a meaningful way at the side of proletarians, when we've stood in a meaningful way at the side of the poor, when we've opposed Capital and Power, when we've opposed the real criminals. It is ridiculous that it is us who were locked up in prison even before trial, it is utterly ridiculous that it is us whose life is jeopardized as we are threatened with being sent back to prison for many years.

I do not consider this court impartial. You are conducting a special trial, in a special courtroom, under special conditions, and you have imposed a ban on media coverage of the proceedings without even allowing a proper recording of minutes, thus rendering the registration of this historical process impossible. This alone shows that there is premeditation in relation to this trial. I believe you have no basis for convicting us for any specific actions—because everyone knows what lack of evidence there is against the three of us (let alone against the other co-accused). Nevertheless, Maziotis, Gournas and I stand trial as "leaders" of the organization, and we will be convicted in the end. The three of us have claimed political responsibility for our participation in Revolutionary Struggle, we have declared that we are proud of our participation, and we will repeat it as many times as necessary. Still, there is no evidence whatsoever tying us to any specific actions.

Regarding the issue of leadership in the organization, I would like to say this: We are anarchists, and as anarchists not only do we not accept hierarchy, but we despise it. Of course, it is also clear to me that no other revolutionary organization active in revolutionary urban guerrilla warfare has a hierarchical structure either.

We fight to banish hierarchy in society. It would be impossible to build an organization that would nurture within its core the same social structures that we are fighting to overthrow. I think that Revolutionary Struggle is in fact a miniature version of what we propose as a model of social organization, i.e. a horizontal organization, without any leaders, without the rulers and the ruled.

You have no basis for convicting us on the charge of "leadership" either, but you will sentence us on these grounds anyway. The decision to include this accusation against the three of us is political. Regarding Gournas, he was labeled a leader in the process; he was not one from the beginning. What does this mean? That by taking political responsibility Gournas was automatically included in those who are allegedly leaders, because he took on the political weight of an organization. I bet that if there were another five claiming political responsibility, they would also be charged with leadership. What would we be talking about then? A horizontal organization of leaders. Is that so?

Another thing I want to emphasize is this: in the whole of Greece it is well known that Maziotis, and I by extension (since we are life companions), have been followed and surveilled since 2002, when my comrade had been released from prison, until recently. There have been many TV shows about this matter. In other words, there was a long-term surveillance of the two of us—mainly Maziotis, but we lived together all these years, so as a result, of me as well—and this did not reveal any evidence about our organization or indeed about anything. I would like to say this: despite the obvious lack of evidence, I believe that ultimately we will be convicted for both leadership and all specific actions. I think that you will issue a political judgment because you will not accept that "these persons come forward, claim political responsibility, publicly speak out about their positions and defend actions of such nature, and we'll let them walk away by simply sentencing them for their participation."

I believe you have orders to convict us. And it is important to point this out: that the court judgment will not only be sentencing us to one hundred years in prison, but it will further set a political precedent. What will this precedent be? That all these "gentlemen," former ministers of Public Order, current and former directors and governors of intelligence agencies and the antiterrorist force, several CIA agents who have tailed us from time to time—for how long I cannot know really—and in any case all secret services of Greece and some from abroad, politicians in Greece, former ministers and by extension the governments themselves are actually quite incapable and powerless in the matter of security. Or, in other words, it will be said, "You had the leaders ever since 2003, when the organization first appeared, you were constantly on their tail watching them, and what did you do? Nothing! They acted unobstructed all these years." So, as "leaders" we went out, organized, carried out actions, wrote proclamations, and lifted the entire burden of an organization, and behind us there were hordes of secret agents and police officers.

These are not just stories from my personal experience. It has all been recorded by TV channels, in their various news shows; it has all been broadcast on radios. And Markogiannakis, former minister of Public Order, had undertaken to bear the entire burden in relation to the surveillance, to defend the secret services in Greece and the antiterrorist force of the Greek police throughout the period preceding our arrests, and he even stated that they did not cease for a minute, tracking our every move.

I will propose the following challenge, and say: bring them here. Call them to the stand. Bring in Markogiannakis; call Korantis; call Chorianopoulos, who is mentioned by Markogiannakis in his interviews; call all these "gentlemen" to testify. Call the former ambassador of the United States in place when the American embassy was attacked. Call the

CIA agents who had us under their surveillance. Bring all these "gentlemen" into this court to publicly admit—this would make me very happy, I assure you—that "we had them under constant surveillance all these years, but we lost track of them for long periods" (because in order to prepare an action of the organization it takes time, it cannot be done in a moment), "they vanished, we did not know their whereabouts, and then attacks were made, and they would suddenly reappear, and we just did not do anything." Call them here to admit that their security measures were shredded by us, that we have put them to complete shame. Let them come here and say this publicly, and I assure you that I myself will accept my involvement in any specific acts they'll refer to. I will also accept the role related to the acts themselves. Bring these people here. It would be my pleasure as a revolutionary that the establishment be humiliated publicly and forced to admit that "we had the specific persons" (this is unprecedented in the history of the revolutionary movement worldwide), "but they managed to make total fools of us and went ahead and did all they did anyway." If this happens, then I can assure you that—apart from my participation in Revolutionary Struggle—I myself will take responsibility for the specific actions, too.

**RAMI SYRIANOS 2012**

RAMI SYRIANOS IS A GREEK ANARCHIST THAT was convicted of robbing a state-run auction house (Organization for Public Property Management, ODDY) in Thessaloniki, Greece, that exists to auction seized vehicles. He was sentenced to 8 years and 8 months in prison, but was released on June 3rd, 2015, after serving 3 years in prison.

---

First of all, I would like to clarify that whatever I will state, is in no case any kind of apology. I do not recognize any political or moral legitimacy in this court, that could motivate me to consider necessary an apology of mine to it.

The entirety of my statement is a public testimony of the political reasoning on which my choice of expropriating the money gathered in the auction of ODDY on the 31st of January 2011, was based.

Before referring to the facts concerning the particular choice of expropriation, there are some things that should be said in order to define the general circumstances where both the expropriation and this court are being placed.

It can no longer be other than clear to anyone, the fact that we're living in an era of turbulence. There's no need for someone to be a sociologist or a financial analyst in order to understand that the social circumstance has since some time ago taken the character of an open conflict. The crackles brought by the financial crisis of 2008, have outreached the sphere of economy and crossed vertically through every aspect of social relations. The shining showcase of capitalism was turned into shivers, revealing behind it the rotting of an—existentially—bankrupt social regime, clinging to life with technical support. The fake well-being image of the previous decades, demystified along with the democratic illusions and the capitalist promises that accompanied it, is being replaced by the image of a dystopian future, where fear and uncertainty prevail, while social coherence, having its impermeability destroyed, gives way to social polarization.

In this explosive situation that is being constructed, where social peace looks like a fairy tale from the past, Dominance throws away every mask and launches an all-out attack. Exploiting the general transitional phase of the social scene, declares a permanent "state of emergency" and adopts a polemical rhetoric. To anyone willing to listen, it's obvious that behind every declaration for more policing and every call for national unity, hides a declaration of war. The new voice of Power is dripping blood and its message is that it will stay alive at all costs. That a new cycle of profitable growth and capital accumulation will open, marching on corpses. In the name of achieving this bloodthirsty Growth, the dominant political and economic complex utilizes all means available. Politicians, journalists, judges, cops, entrepreneurs, prison guards, financial analysts, sociologists, in short, each and every individual faithful to the system, place themselves with heart and mind into saving the empire of profit. While the political and financial

sharks organize the new terms of poverty, through over-in-
tensification of work, exterminating taxation and commercial-
ization even of the last trace of human life, the police state
is being established with the blessings of the Media. Public
life is getting militarized with the omnipresent mercenaries of
police, while new anti-terrorist laws, biological databases. and
surveillance systems are being used for protection against the
internal enemy that threatens the fragile social equilibrium.
Repression is being lifted as the central axis of social mechan- ·
ics and broadens its targets. Every radical action is being criminalized, while persecutions of conscience, incarcerations, and
political pogroms complete the dogma of zero tolerance. Every
aspect of life is being attacked by the mechanical functions of
the social regime that wraps firmly into a new form of total-
itarianism. Within this belligerent situation, every aspect of
existence is being converted into a sometimes individual and
sometimes collective battlefield. Every person is called to take
a stand, every minute.

While the ones in Power sweat to build the new totalitarian
world order, along with their minions and the social canni-
balism, selfishness and fascism are being consolidated, a whole
galaxy of individual and collective practices of resistance is
being developed in geometrical progress. In the city's streets
at night, inside hideouts and squatted public spaces, people
with different experiences and starting points are getting coor-
dinated while setting their selves into the multiform procedure of social liberation. Relentless dynamic demonstrations,
guerrilla attacks, self-organized solidarity structures, illegal
wildcat strikes, collective expropriation of goods, sabotage,
denials of payment and occupations of public spaces and buildings, together with uncountable other practices, compose the
entire mosaic of a revolutionary procedure in development. A
community of people is being built upon the conscience of
rebellion and proposes by word and acts that the bet for the

liberation of the human experience from the degeneration of oppression, is still on.

An organic part of this community of people, is the multiform anarchist movement into which I place myself. During my political trajectory, I have participated in various aspects of the anarchist movement, always seeking for thought and paths of action that would contribute in the best way to the subversive process. Through this course of mine, I have fumbled and I keep on grasping at the different pieces of the mosaic of negations that make up the subversive anarchist vision. A vision that maintained the clarity of the revolutionary perspective intact, both in the dark years of repression and in the years of assimilation and conformity. That kept the unity between theory and action, personal and political intact, rejecting the bourgeois capitalist logic which fragments the human existence into seemingly independent and separate fields.

Carrying this precise awareness of the inseparable unity between perception and action, theory and daily life, I cannot imagine how I could perceive the current social situation as oppressing and enslaving, without fighting by all means for its subversion. How could I perceive the dominant relations as alienated and empty, without trying to create substantial, expropriated relationships of solidarity with the people around me. How could I perceive waged labor as a blackmailing procedure of inequalities, without acting towards individual and collective liberation?

My choice to expropriate the money gathered in the ODDY auction, makes up my individual answer in this last dilemma. Denying for myself the roles of both worker and boss, exploiter or exploited, I decided to put into active practice my opposition to waged labor, attacking a parasitic fence organization of the State.

If someone wants to understand the motives behind this choice of mine, they only have to reflect upon their own daily life. The feeling of emptiness and encapsulation created by the repetitive routine of the working timetables and the pre-fixed routes. The isolation, boredom, loneliness and insecurity that one feels when left alone at home, exhausted. From the morning wake-up to the night's consumption, life is getting crushed inside the belligerent situation of the waged blackmail. And if someone thinks that terms like "belligerent situation" are used to impress, they just need to consider even the most modest and conservative statistics in relation to the cost of waged labor upon human life, in order to confirm beyond any doubt the literalness of this expression. In Greece alone, one worker dies every three days. Globally, more than 2 million people die every year by some workplace accident. And there's no statistics, of course, about how many people suffer from depression, how many have been led to psychoactive pills or drugs, trying to fight the absence of meaning in the schizoid circle of production and consumption. There are no statistics about the suicides that this constant, low-tension war has provoked.

Nowadays, with labor being totally demystified, few are those who do not realize its true nature. People all over the world, every day turn their will into action, to act against the nature of work, negating in total, or just for some moments, their role as human components within this globalized profit machine. Sabotages on production lines, destructions at work spaces, fake illnesses in order to avoid work, stealing from bosses, deliberate under-productivity, expropriating raids upon accumulated wealth, are all aspects of the common disgust produced for work, in anyone that has worked even for an hour in their lives. Practices of resistance within a procedure that degenerates the human existence into a sequence of automated acts and thoughts.

So, these are the motives of this act of mine.

I am here to be judged as a thief, by a court which—under the disguise of morality and justice—undertakes the task of legitimizing a social regime that systematically and ruthlessly robs the very existence of the people. By a court, the substantial existence of which, is the preservation and the perpetuation of oppression and inequality.

I'm here in order to be judged as a public danger, in front of a justice which constantly prefers to exhaust its cruelty and hatred upon every marginalized person, any outcast, any stranger. A justice whose mission is to place the last stone in the fortress of terror that Dominance builds around itself. That criminalizes friendship and comradely relationships, throwing heavy condemnations at every fighting person, creates new anti-terrorist laws that could encompass anyone, persecutes people because of their political identity.

I am standing here as anarchist and revolutionary human, against this justice of yours. Against the totality of the dominant financial and political complex that is the definition of barbarity and which you express.

I am standing here for my decision to release myself from this wretched and necrotic reality that is presented as moral and legal.

Finally, I am standing here because I consciously chose to steal time from the production process, and money from the State's machine, in order to allocate them into the final destruction of both.

With regards to this choice of mine, I declare myself strongly unrepentant.

**OLGA NUCLEUS 2013**

IN MARCH 2011, AN EARTHQUAKE AND SUBSEQUENT tsunami caused damage to the nuclear power plant at Fukushima, Japan. The damage caused a nuclear meltdown, that to this day hasn't been fully contained. More than eight years later the plant has continued to leak radioactive water into the Pacific Ocean.

In May 2012 Roberto Adinolfi, the managing director of Ansaldo Nucleare, was shot in the leg. Ansaldo Nucleare is a nuclear power company owned by Finmeccanica. Finmeccanica S.p.A. is the leading industrial group in the high technology sector in Italy and one of the main global players in aerospace, defense, and security. It operates in seven sectors: aeronautics, helicopters, space, electronics, defense systems, energy, transportation, and construction. The shooting was claimed by the Olga Nucleus of the Informal Anarchist Federation (FAI).

In November 2013 two anarchists were convicted of the shooting. Alfredo Cospito was sentenced to 9 years, 5 months and 10 days in prison, while Nicola Gai received 8 years, 8 months, 20 days, after a reduction from the original sentences.

*"It is true that Cospito and Gai today have confessed,"* said Prosecutor Nicola Piacente. *"But the second part of the confession is still missing. They have not disowned (what they did), on the contrary, they disrespect authority and the law."*

...dreams are to be realized here and now, not in a hypothetical future, because the future has always been sold by priests of whatever religion or ideology in order to steal from us with impunity. We want a present worth living and not simply sacrificed to the messianic expectation of a future earthly paradise. For this reason we wanted to talk of an anarchy to be realized now and not in the future. The "everything now" is a bet, a game we play where the stakes are our lives, everybody's life, and our death, everybody's death...
—Pierleone Mario Porcu

Science is the eternal sacrifice of life, fleeting, ephemeral but real, on the altar of eternal abstractions. What I predict is therefore the revolt of life against the government of science.
—Mikhail Bakunin

Even while he stalked a God in his own fancy, an infantine imbecility came over him... Art—the Arts—arose supreme, and, once enthroned, cast chains upon the intellect which had elevated them to power.—Edgar Allan Poe

The empire that reigns sovereign founded on nothing is collapsing
It cannot bear the weight of truth
I recommend a massive dose of life!

I recommend a massive dose of life!
At least that way you will be able to say you have
lived it. —Congegno

Bastards...I know who sent you!!!
—Roberto Adinolfi

IN A WONDERFUL MORNING IN MAY I ACTED, AND IN THE SPACE
of a few hours I fully enjoyed my life. For once I left fear and
self-justification behind and defied the unknown. In a Europe
dotted with nuclear power stations, one of those mainly responsible for the nuclear disaster to come fell at my feet. I want to

**ALFREDO
COSPITO**
be absolutely clear: the Olga FAI/FRI nucleus
is only Nicola and I. No one else took part in
this action, or helped, or planned it. Nobody
knew about our project.

I won't allow my action to be placed within an obscene and
absurd media and judicial cauldron in order to divert attention
from its real goal, a cauldron made of 'subversion of the democratic order', 'conspiracy', 'armed gang', 'terrorism': empty
words that fill the mouths of judges and journalists.

I am an anti-organization anarchist because I oppose all
forms of authority and organizational constraints. I am nihilist
because I live my anarchy today and not in waiting for a revolution, which—if it ever came about—would only produce
more authority, technology, civilization. I live my anarchy with
ease, joy, pleasure, without any spirit of martyrdom, by oppos-
ing this civilized existence with all my strength, an existence I
cannot bear. I am antisocial because I am convinced that society
can only exist in the differentiation between the dominant and
the dominated. I do not strive for any future blissful socialist
alchemy, I do not trust any social class; my revolt without revolution is individual, existential, overpowering, absolute, armed.

There's no feeling of omnipotence in me, no disdain for the

oppressed, for the "people." As an eastern saying goes: "Don't scorn the snake because it doesn't have horns; one day it might turn into a dragon!" Similarly a slave can turn into a rebel, one man or one woman can become devastating fire. I scorn the powerful of the earth with all my strength, be they politicians, scientists, technocrats, leaders of all sorts, bureaucrats, army and religious chiefs.

The order I want to knock down is that of civilization, which destroys everything that makes life worth living day by day. State, democracy, social classes, ideologies, religions, police, armies, your very court, are shadows, ghosts, cogs of an all-embracing mega-machine that can be replaced. One day technology will do without us and will transform us all into atoms lost in a landscape of death and desolation.

On that 7th May 2012 I threw sand in the cogs of this mega-machine in the space of a second, and during that second I fully lived and made a difference. On that day my weapon was not an old Tokarev (a type of pistol —ed.) but the deep and ferocious hatred I feel towards techno-industrial society. I claimed the action as FAI/FRI because I fell in love with this lucid "madness" that has become true poetry, at times a breeze, at others a storm, blowing halfway around the world, undaunted, improbable, against all laws, "commonsense," ideologies, politics, science and civilization, against all authorities, organizations and hierarchies.

A concrete view of anarchy that doesn't contemplate theoreticians, leaders, cadres, soldiers, heroes, martyrs, organization charts, militants or spectators. For years I had been witnessing the development of this new anarchy as a spectator. For too long I'd been looking on. If anarchy doesn't turn into action it rejects life and becomes ideology, shit or a little more, in the best of cases a powerless outburst of frustrated men and women.

I decided to go for action after the nuclear disaster in Fukushima. Far too often we feel impotent in the face of such big events. Primitive men faced danger, they knew how to defend themselves. Civilized and modern men are helpless in the face of the constructions-constraints of technology.

Just as sheep look at the shepherd for protection, the very shepherd that will slaughter them, so we civilized men confide in the secular priests of science, the very priests that are slowly digging our grave.

We saw Adinolfi smiling slyly and playing the victim from television screens. We saw him lecturing against "terrorism" in schools. But I wonder: what is terrorism? A gunshot, a searing pain, an open wound, or the incessant, continuous threat of a slow death devouring you from inside? The continuous incessant terror that one of their nuclear plants can vomit death and desolation upon us all of a sudden?

Ansaldo Nucleare and Finmeccanica bear huge responsibilities. Their projects continue to sow death everywhere. Recently the rumour has spread of probable investments in the enlargement of the nuclear plant of Kryko, Slovenia, a high seismic risk area very close to Italy. In Cernadova, Romania, several incidents have occurred since 2000, caused by Ansaldo's stupidity during the construction of one of their plants. How many lives have been lost? How much blood shed? Technocrats of Anslado and Finmeccanica, all facile smiles and a "clean" conscience: your "progress" stinks of death, and the death you sow all over the world is shouting for revenge.

There are many ways to effectively oppose nuclear power: blockades of trains carrying nuclear waste, sabotage of the pylons carrying electricity produced by nuclear power. I had the idea of striking the one most responsible for this mess in Italy: Roberto Adinolfi, managing director of Ansaldo Nucleare. It didn't take much to find out where he lived, five sessions of lying in wait were sufficient. There's no need for a military structure, a subversive association or an armed gang in order to strike. Anyone armed with a strong will can think the unthinkable and act consequently. I'd have liked to have done it all by myself but unfortunately I needed help with the bike. I asked Nicola and appealed to his friendship. He didn't back down. I bought the gun for three hundred euro on the black market. There's no need for clandestine infrastructures or huge amounts of money to arm oneself. We left by car from Turin the night before. Everything went smoothly, or kind of. Nicola was driving. I struck right where we had decided to strike. An accurate shot, I ran towards the bike and then the unexpected, the angry cry of Adinolfi, the shouted sentence that froze me: 'Bastards...I know who sent you!'

At that very moment I had the absolute certainty that I had hit the target, and was fully aware that I had put my hands into a cesspit: money interests, international finance, politics and power, mud and cesspit. Those "stolen" seconds allowed Adinolfi to read a part of the number plate, which we hadn't covered due to inexperience. Thanks to the numbers they traced the bike, and then the camera.

It won't be the sentence of this court to turn us into bad terrorists and Adinolfi and Finmeccanica benefactors of humanity. The time has come for the great refusal, a refusal made of a plurality of resistance, each of them special. Some are possible, necessary, improbable; others are spontaneous, wild, solitary, arranged, overflowing or violent. Ours was solitary and violent. Was it worthwhile? Yes! If only for the joy we felt when we heard of the defiant smile that Olga Ikonomidou, brave sister of the Conspiracy of Cells of Fire, threw in the face of her jailers from a solitary confinement cell of a Greek prison.

I'm happy to be what I am, a free man even if I'm "temporarily" in chains. I can't complain much, given that the vast majority of "people" have chains well placed in their brains. I've always tried to do what I thought right and never what was convenient. Half measures never convinced me. I've loved a lot. Hated a lot. And for that reason I won't surrender to your bars, uniforms, weapons. You'll always find me an irreducible, proud enemy. But not just me. Anarchists are never alone, sometimes they are solitary but never alone. A thousand projects in our minds, a hope in our hearts that stays alive, stronger and stronger, determined and shared more and more. A concrete perspective that 'risks' changing the face of anarchy in the world. Small, great earthquakes that will stir a cataclysm one day. It will take time, never mind, for the time being I am enjoying the earthquake that broke out inside me from all this desire for joy and struggle.

I conclude with a quotation from Marco Camenisch, unconquered warrior, prisoner for over 20 years because of his profound love of life, today locked up in a filthy Swiss prison. I make his words my own:

> '...the courage to think things through, to break the technological police bans of the "impossible" and the "unconceivable", the courage to thinking other and in another way act consequently. Only this can take us beyond the tepid toxic dishwater of modernity into places where nothing and nobody will lead us, to a place without security, the place of responsibility in first person, for non-submission with all its consequences. Freedom is hard and dangerous and there's no life without death. For fear of losing our lives we often surrender to slavery and annihilation.'

Death to civilization
Death to technological society
Long live the CCF
Long live the FAI/FRI
Long live the black international!
*Lunga vita all'anarchia!*

💣

> Nobody can judge me
> Not even you
> The truth hurts you, I know.—C. Caselli

A few words to make a few simple points before the "truth" is pronounced by the court; just in case it's not clear, I am using the word "truth" ironically as I don't recognize any tribunal other than my own conscience. The only ones responsible for what happened in Genoa on May 7, 2012 are Alfredo and **NICOLA** myself. None of our friends or comrades knew what **GAI** we were planning and then carried out. No matter how far you dig into our lives and relations to find accomplices of the "crime," you won't be able to demonstrate anything to the contrary; of course you'll try but it'll be a lie and an attempt to incriminate some enemy of the existent. I understand that those who have dedicated all their lives to serving authority won't find it easy to accept the idea that two individuals, armed only with their determination, could decide to try to jam the gears of the techno-industrial system instead of contributing to running it in a disciplined way; but that's just how it is. After years spent witnessing the systematic destruction of nature and all the aspects that make life worth living carried out by the never too highly praised technological development. Years spent following with interest, but always as a spectator, the experiences of the rebels who, even in this seemingly pacified world, continue to raise their heads and affirm the possibility of a free and wild life. Following the Fukushima disaster, when Alfredo proposed that I help him carry out an action against Roberto Adinolfi, I accepted without thinking twice. At last I could concretely demonstrate my refusal of the techno-industrial system, and put an end to participating in symbolic protests that far too often are just demonstrations of powerlessness. Nobody with even the slightest intelligence can deceive themselves that the result of a referendum or the clowning of some green economy guru can erase even just the most harmful aspects of the world we are forced to live in. Anyone who wants to can see that Finmeccanica and its subsidiary [Ansaldo Nucleare, TN] continue to produce weapons of mass destruction; they simply do this beyond the Italian borders, as if radiation respected these vile barriers.

In Romania (Cernadova, an unfortunate area known mainly for countless incidents at its nuclear plant), Slovakia and the Ukraine, to mention just the most recent and direct investments, Ansaldo Nucleare continues to spread death and to contribute to the destruction of nature. As should be obvious to everybody, with another 190 nuclear power stations in Europe alone, the problem is not wondering if another Chernobyl *might* occur, but *when* it will. And moreover, we mustn't forget that these monstrosities don't just kill when they are functioning, but also do so with their nuclear waste. This is transported back and forth all over Europe with nobody knowing what to do with it. The nuclear waste from the Italian power stations, closed down decades ago, is now being transported to France in order to be made "safe": they get fuel from it to supply more nuclear reactors, and also a few kilos of plutonium that can only be used to make bombs (just to remind us that there's no difference between military and civil use as far as nuclear power is concerned), then the waste is sent back as dangerous as it was before. On this question, who knows what the Americans will do with the uranium that was secretly transferred to the USA in the summer from a nuclear waste site in Basilicata. I could talk about the damage and destruction caused by nuclear power for hours, give countless examples, go over what's going on in Fukushima (where some are saying that no deaths were caused by the nuclear power station...) but I'm not here to seek justification. Perhaps nuclear power is the one element of this civilized world where the senseless monstrosity of the techno-industrial system can be understood by anybody, but we have to realize that we are sacrificing all protection of our individual freedom and the chance to live a worthwhile life on the altar of technological development. Now it is up to each one of us to decide whether we want to be obedient subjects or whether we want to try to live, here and now, the refusal of the existent. I have made up my mind, with joy and with no remorse.

We'll get out of here branded as terrorists, the amusing thing is that you can say that without seeming ridiculous: it is what the law states. One thing sure is that words have lost all their meaning; if we are terrorists, what would you call those who produce weapons, tracking systems for missiles, drones, fighter-bombers, equipment to hunt people trying to cross borders, nuclear power stations, those who do deals with assassins in uniform and famous dictators, in other words, how would you define Finmeccanica? Well, your bosses certainly don't have much imagination, so much so that in order to dispel any doubts about the real function of this company they recently appointed former policeman Gianni De Gennaro company director: given his responsibility for the torture at Bolzaneto and the massacre at the Diaz when he was police chief at the time of the G8 of 2001, they naturally thought that he was the right man in the right place.

To get back to the reasons for this declaration of mine I'd like to make a few points about the "brilliant" operation that led to our arrest. Who knows how many handshakes and pats on the back for the cunning hounds that managed to exploit our one, but fatal, mistake due to inexperience and the urgency to do something after the Fukushima disaster. In fact we didn't notice a CCTV camera placed by a zealous bar owner in order to protect his sandwiches. Unfortunately for us, we didn't see it when we were studying the route from the spot where we left the moped and the bus stop where we changed buses and reached the city suburbs in the direction of Arenzano where my car, that we used to go to Genoa and come back, was parked. To tell the truth, the camera was not our only mistake, we also lost precious moments when we were leaving the place of the action, as the angry shout of the apprentice sorcerer of nuclear power: "Bastards, I know who sent you!" froze us. It's not up to me to jump to conclusions about the meaning of that sentence, it wasn't the right moment for calm thinking, nor am I in the habit of building castles in the air out of someone else's words, but personally I drew the conclusion that we had put our hands on a pile of shit. Everything else used to justify our detention is either distorted or simply false. The famous piece of phone tapping about the "big pistol," where I allegedly stated I fired the shot, is totally unintelligible; there's no point in getting experts involved to dismantle it, but as I was driving the moped it would have been impossible for me to also be holding the pistol, just as it seems logically absurd to me that I would be saying this to precisely the person who had taken part in the action with me, i.e. Alfredo.

As for the printer that was seized from my parents' house, which the forensic scientist stated was the one used to print the leaflet, it's not even worth talking about. I bought the computer and printer and we destroyed them both after using them (it should be noted that after the court of review reconfirmed our arrest, even the scientists of the RIS [Scientific Investigations Department —ed.] realized that the seized printer was not the one used for the leaflet). As far as the theft of the moped is concerned, which we are accused of along with non-existent "unknown persons," things are not as complicated as your efforts to recreate them. We went around the city trying to solve the problem, as we had no experience of this kind of thing. As we know, good luck favours the brave, and in the pleasant locality of Bolzaneto we bumped into a scooter with the keys still in the ignition; we took them and decided to go back a few days later with a helmet. The bike was still in the same place, I just got on it, started the engine and drove it to the vicinity of the Staglieno cemetery, where it remained parked until fifteen days before the action, when I moved it closer to Mr Adinolfi's house. I apologize to the owner for removing the helmets and other objects that were under the seat and for throwing away the back trunk, these objects would have been obstacles to the action and certainly it wouldn't have been a good idea to have tried to get them back. Another element that the investigators have embellished and, I'm afraid, will try to use in their role as good inquisitors in the future, is some phone tapping by the CSL in Naples, where some comrades allegedly commented on the leaflet they allegedly got via e-mail as a world first. I don't know what they are talking about, I won't go into how difficult it is to understand the dialogue, to say the least, nor is there any point in dwelling on the obvious consonance between "*Valentino*" and "*volantino*" ["leaflet" in Italian], but I do know for sure that the communiqué was only sent via ordinary mail (we posted the letters during the change of buses on our way back, in a post box on the seafront near the ferry terminal), so it is impossible for the comrades to have received it via e-mail.

I know for sure that you will use our case to make an example, that your revenge will be draconian, that you will do anything to keep us isolated (suffice it to say that our letters have been subjected to censorship for more than a year), but I want to give you some bad news: your efforts will be in vain. For at least 150 years judges, even more ferocious than yourselves, have been trying to erase the idea of the possibility of a life free from authority, but with poor results. I can calmly assure you that your repressive actions, no matter how wide and indiscriminate, won't be able to disarticulate or eradicate anything.

If you think that, thanks to us, you will be able to track other anarchists who have decided to put the chaotic, spontaneous and informal possibilities of the FAI to the test, you are

absolutely mistaken and you will draw a blank, like always; neither Alfredo or myself know anyone who has made this choice.
You are chasing a ghost that you can't lock up in the petty
procedures of your legal codes. That is because it manifests
itself in the instant in which the destructive tensions of those
who animate it come together in order to act, in the instant
when free women and men decide to put anarchy concretely
to the test. Now that the experience of the Olga Nucleus is
concluded I can only assure you that I have found new reasons
to feed my hatred and motives to desire the destruction of the
world composed of authority, exploitation, and the devastation
of nature.

Love and complicity to the sisters and brothers who make
the mad dream of the FAI/FRI real with their actions all over
the world.

Love and complicity to the comrades who, anonymously or
not, continue to attack in the name of the possibility of a life
free from authority.

Love and freedom to all anarchist prisoners.

Long live the black international of the rebels against the
deadly order of civilization.

*Lunga vita all'anarchia!*

Jeremy Hammond

## JEREMY HAMMOND 2013

JEREMY HAMMOND IS A US-BASED ANARCHIST hacker and member of the Anonymous hacking collective. Arrested ten times between the ages of 18 and 21, Hammond was then sentenced to two years in federal prison following his hack of the website of briefly popular right-wing patriot group Protest Warrior. In 2013, Hammond was sentenced to a ten-year prison term (the maximum possible) for hacking into the database of private intelligence company Stratfor. This operation was done purely with the guidance and support of a hacker that had been turned informant by the FBI, named Sabu. As of this writing, Jeremy has less than a year left to serve, but has been called before a Grand Jury, the same Grand Jury that Chelsea Manning is currently refusing to testify before. Jeremy is also refusing to testify.

——————————————————

Good morning. Thank you for this opportunity. My name is Jeremy Hammond and I'm here to be sentenced for hacking activities carried out during my involvement with Anonymous.

I have been locked up at MCC [Metropolitan Correctional Center, in New York City —ed.] for the past 20 months and have had a lot of time to think about how I would explain my actions

Before I begin, I want to take a moment to recognize the work of the people who have supported me. I want to thank all the lawyers and others who worked on my case: Elizabeth Fink, Susan Kellman, Sarah Kunstler, Emily Kunstler, Margaret Kunstler, and Grainne O'Neill. I also want to thank the National Lawyers Guild, the Jeremy Hammond Defense Committee and Support Network, Free Anons, the Anonymous Solidarity Network, Anarchist Black Cross, and all others who have helped me by writing a letter of support, sending me letters, attending my court dates, and spreading the word about my case. I also want to shout out my brothers and sisters behind bars and those who are still out there fighting the power.

The acts of civil disobedience and direct action that I am being sentenced for today are in line with the principles of community and equality that have guided my life. I hacked into dozens of high profile corporations and government institutions, understanding very clearly that what I was doing was against the law, and that my actions could land me back in federal prison. But I felt that I had an obligation to use my skills to expose and confront injustice—and to bring the truth to light

Could I have achieved the same goals through legal means? I have tried everything from voting and petitions to peaceful protest and have found that those in power do not want the truth to be exposed. When we speak truth to power we are ignored at best and brutally suppressed at worst. We are confronting a power structure that does not respect its own system of checks and balances, never mind the rights of it's own citizens or the international community.

My introduction to politics was when George W. Bush stole

the Presidential election in 2000, then took advantage of the waves of racism and patriotism after 9/11 to launch unprovoked imperialist wars against Iraq and Afghanistan. I took to the streets in protest naively believing our voices would be heard in Washington and we could stop the war. Instead, we were labeled as traitors, beaten, and arrested.

I have been arrested for numerous acts of civil disobedience on the streets of Chicago, but it wasn't until 2005 that I used my computer skills to break the law in political protest. I was arrested by the FBI for hacking into the computer systems of a right-wing, pro-war group called Protest Warrior, an organization that sold racist t-shirts on their website and harassed anti-war groups. I was charged under the Computer Fraud and Abuse Act, and the "intended loss" in my case was arbitrarily calculated by multiplying the 5000 credit cards in Protest Warrior's database by $500, resulting in a total of $2.5 million.

My sentencing guidelines were calculated on the basis of this "loss," even though not a single credit card was used or distributed by me or anyone else. I was sentenced to two years in prison.

While in prison I have seen for myself the ugly reality of how the criminal justice system destroys the lives of the millions of people held captive behind bars. The experience solidified my opposition to repressive forms of power and the importance of standing up for what you believe.

When I was released, I was eager to continue my involvement in struggles for social change. I didn't want to go back to prison, so I focused on above-ground community organizing. But over time, I became frustrated with the limitations of peaceful protest, seeing it as reformist and ineffective. The Obama administration continued the wars in Iraq and Afghanistan, escalated the use of drones, and failed to close Guantanamo Bay.

Around this time, I was following the work of groups like

Wikileaks and Anonymous. It was very inspiring to see the ideas of hactivism coming to fruition. I was particularly moved by the heroic actions of Chelsea Manning, who had exposed the atrocities committed by US forces in Iraq and Afghanistan. She took an enormous personal risk to leak this information— believing that the public had a right to know and hoping that her disclosures would be a positive step to end these abuses. It is heart-wrenching to hear about her cruel treatment in military lockup.

I thought long and hard about choosing this path again. I had to ask myself, if Chelsea Manning fell into the abysmal nightmare of prison fighting for the truth, could I in good conscience do any less, if I was able? I thought the best way to demonstrate solidarity was to continue the work of exposing and confronting corruption.

I was drawn to Anonymous because I believe in autonomous, decentralized direct action. At the time Anonymous was involved in operations in support of the Arab Spring uprisings, against censorship, and in defense of Wikileaks. I had a lot to contribute, including technical skills, and how to better articulate ideas and goals. It was an exciting time - the birth of a digital dissent movement, where the definitions and capabilities of hacktivism were being shaped.

I was especially interested in the work of the hackers of LulzSec who were breaking into some significant targets and becoming increasingly political. Around this time, I first started talking to Sabu, who was very open about the hacks he supposedly committed, and was encouraging hackers to unite and attack major government and corporate systems under the banner of Anti Security. But very early in my involvement, the other Lulzsec hackers were arrested, leaving me to break into systems and write press releases. Later, I would learn that Sabu had been the first one arrested, and that the entire time I was talking to him he was an FBI informant.

Anonymous was also involved in the early stages of Occupy Wall Street. I was regularly participating on the streets as part of Occupy Chicago and was very excited to see a worldwide mass movement against the injustices of capitalism and racism. In several short months, the 'Occupations' came to an end, closed by police crackdowns and mass arrests of protestors who were kicked out of their own public parks. The repression of Anonymous and the Occupy Movement set the tone for Antisec in the following months—the majority of our hacks against police targets were in retaliation for the arrests of our comrades.

I targeted law enforcement systems because of the racism and inequality with which the criminal law is enforced. I targeted the manufacturers and distributors of military and police equipment who profit from weaponry used to advance US political and economic interests abroad and to repress people at home. I targeted information security firms because they work in secret to protect government and corporate interests at the expense of individual rights, undermining and discrediting activists, journalists and other truth seekers, and spreading disinformation.

I had never even heard of Stratfor until Sabu brought it to my attention. Sabu was encouraging people to invade systems, and helping to strategize and facilitate attacks. He even provided me with vulnerabilities of targets passed on by other hackers, so it came as a great surprise when I learned that Sabu had been working with the FBI the entire time.

On December 4, 2011, Sabu was approached by another hacker who had already broken into Stratfor's credit card database. Sabu, under the watchful eye of his government handlers, then brought the hack to Antisec by inviting this hacker to our private chatroom, where he supplied download links to the full credit card database as well as the initial vulnerability access point to Stratfor's systems.

I spent some time researching Stratfor and reviewing the information we were given, and decided that their activities and client base made them a deserving target. I did find it ironic that Stratfor's wealthy and powerful customer base had their credit cards used to donate to humanitarian organizations, but my main role in the attack was to retrieve Stratfor's private email spools which is where all the dirty secrets are typically found.

It took me more than a week to gain further access into Stratfor's internal systems, but I eventually broke into their mail server. There was so much information, we needed several servers of our own in order to transfer the emails. Sabu, who was involved with the operation at every step, offered a server, which was provided and monitored by the FBI. Over the next weeks, the emails were transferred, the credit cards were used for donations, and Stratfor's systems were defaced and destroyed. Why the FBI would introduce us to the hacker who found the initial vulnerability and allow this hack to continue remains a mystery.

As a result of the Stratfor hack, some of the dangers of the unregulated private intelligence industry are now known. It has been revealed through Wikileaks and other journalists around the world that Stratfor maintained a worldwide network of informants that they used to engage in intrusive and possibly illegal surveillance activities on behalf of large multinational corporations.

After Stratfor, I continued to break into other targets, using a powerful "zero day exploit" allowing me administrator access to systems running the popular Plesk webhosting platform. Sabu asked me many times for access to this exploit, which I refused to give him. Without his own independent access, Sabu continued to supply me with lists of vulnerable targets. I broke into numerous websites he supplied, uploaded the stolen email accounts and databases onto Sabu's FBI server, and handed over passwords and backdoors that enabled Sabu (and, by extension, his FBI handlers) to control these targets.

Sabu also supplied lists of targets that were vulnerable to "zero day exploits" used to break into systems, including a powerful remote root vulnerability effecting the popular Plesk software. At his request, these websites were broken into, their emails and databases were uploaded to Sabu's FBI server, and the password information and the location of root backdoors were supplied. These intrusions took place in January/February of 2012 and affected over 2000 domains, including numerous foreign government websites in Brazil, Turkey, Syria, Puerto Rico, Colombia, Nigeria, Iran, Slovenia, Greece, Pakistan, and others. A few of the compromised websites that I recollect include the official website of the Governor of Puerto Rico, the Internal Affairs Division of the Military Police of Brazil, the Official Website of the Crown Prince of Kuwait, the Tax Department of Turkey, the Iranian Academic Center for Education and Cultural Research, the Polish Embassy in the UK, and the Ministry of Electricity of Iraq.

Sabu also infiltrated a group of hackers that had access to hundreds of Syrian systems including government institutions, banks, and ISPs. He logged several relevant IRC channels persistently asking for live access to mail systems and bank transfer details. The FBI took advantage of hackers who wanted to help support the Syrian people against the Assad regime, who instead unwittingly provided the US government access to Syrian systems, undoubtedly supplying useful intelligence to the military and their buildup for war.

All of this happened under the control and supervision of the FBI and can be easily confirmed by chat logs the government provided to us pursuant to the government's discovery obligations in the case against me. However, the full extent of the FBI's abuses remains hidden. Because I pled guilty, I do not have access to many documents that might have been provided to me in advance of trial, such as Sabu's communications with the FBI. In addition, the majority of the documents provided to me are under a "protective order" which insulates this material from public scrutiny. As government transparency is an issue at the heart of my case, I ask that this evidence be made public. I believe the documents will show that the government's actions go way beyond catching hackers and stopping computer crimes.

The government celebrates my conviction and imprisonment, hoping that it will close the door on the full story. I took responsibility for my actions, by pleading guilty, but when will the government be made to answer for its crimes?

The US hypes the threat of hackers in order to justify the multibillion dollar cybersecurity industrial complex, but it is also responsible for the same conduct it aggressively prosecutes and claims to work to prevent. The hypocrisy of law and order and the injustices caused by capitalism cannot be cured by institutional reform but through civil disobedience and direct action. Yes I broke the law, but I believe that sometimes laws must be broken in order to make room for change.

In the immortal words of Frederick Douglas, "Power concedes nothing without a demand. It never did and it never will. Find out just what any people will quietly submit to and you have found out the exact measure of injustice and wrong which will be imposed upon them, and these will continue till they are resisted with either words or blows, or both. The limits of tyrants are prescribed by the endurance of those whom they oppress."

This is not to say that I do not have any regrets. I realize that I released the personal information of innocent people who had nothing to do with the operations of the institutions I targeted. I apologize for the release of data that was harmful to individuals and irrelevant to my goals. I believe in the individual right to privacy—from government surveillance, and from actors like myself, and I appreciate the irony of my own involvement in the trampling of these rights. I am committed to working to make this world a better place for all of us. I still believe in the importance of hactivism as a form of civil disobedience, but it is time for me to move on to other ways of seeking change. My time in prison has taken a toll on my family, friends, and community. I know I am needed at home. I recognize that 7 years ago I stood before a different federal judge, facing similar charges, but this does not lessen the sincerity of what I say to you today.

It has taken a lot for me to write this, to explain my actions, knowing that doing so—honestly—could cost me more years of my life in prison. I am aware that I could get as many as 10 years, but I hope that I do not, as I believe there is so much work to be done.

Eric King

**ERIC KING 2016**

ERIC KING IS A VEGAN ANARCHIST FROM KANSAS City, Missouri. In 2016 he was convicted of using "explosive materials to commit arson of property used in or affecting interstate commerce" after he threw a hammer through a state representative's office window, followed by two Molotov cocktails, in solidarity with the uprising in Ferguson, Missouri after the murder of Michael Brown by Ferguson Officer Darren Wilson. After a non-cooperating plea deal, King was sentenced to ten years in prison, despite the fact that both Molotov cocktail's failed to ignite.

During his incarceration, King has faced a large amount of repression, spending large amounts of time in segregation, being denied books and visits, being assaulted by guards, and clearly set up for assault by fascist prisoners because of his antifascist tattoo. He is scheduled for release in 2023, though as of press time he is now facing further charges after he was assaulted by a guard.

---

First I'd like to congratulate the Court on such a stellar job. Another graffiti homeless person is off the street. So I'm sure the FBI and Patrick are very proud of themselves. This is a good picture for the United States and they needed this. This is a solid win. You do an amazing job up there.

This is supposed to be a chance for me to speak. I didn't speak this entire time. You've held sentencing and punishment over me, and even now no matter what I say you can still hold that against me, not let me do things, not recommend things. That's such a farce. This whole court's a farce.

I stated what I did. I'm happy I did it. The government in this country is disgusting. The way they treat poor people, the way they treat brown people, the way they treat everyone that's not in the class of white and male is disgusting, patriarchal, filthy racist.

You're all a part of this. From the man over there who works the same corporation company that ran Prime Health Pro (ph) to you that takes away freedom and tears apart the community. You do that thinking that this is justice. This is no justice in ripping people from their homes. For what? Breaking a window? Ten years for breaking a window? And the cop that killed Freddie Gray got zero? The people that killed Trayvon Martin got zero? It's so horrendous.

And I'm not sorry for what I did. I'm sorry that I got caught before I could do more things. I would have loved to attack more government buildings and make sure that bubble of safety that prosecutors and FBI agents and judges feel got shattered so that they stay in their safe pockets knowing they can't touch me even though there are consequences to my actions. Same way we have consequences for our actions. If I throw a hammer at a window, I get ten years in jail. If you sentence a first-time offender to life in prison if he sold meth, you get a clap on the back from the President and a job for life. And if that's justice, then you're use of justice is so skewed and just horrendously immoral.

Further, this isn't a victory for the State. This isn't a win for any of you, any of you on this other side of the table. It's done nothing but affirm my views, affirm my beliefs that the government is just disgusting. Even when I walk in I can't tell my wife I love her. I can't look at her and smile because, what, I broke a window? That's justice? That's fair? That's not justice. There's no rehabilitation in that. There's no freedom in that. There's no constitutional rights in that. It's just bullying. It's just the upper class saying we're going to keep people who did not agree to our rules and then decide not to live by them, we're going to keep those people shackled up so we can live comfortably in our own little bubbles and we never have to look outside of those bubbles to realize what's really happening, which this class is set up to keep people down, and when people step out of that class system, they get punished horrendously, more than any other country, any other country on earth, the land of the free. It's despicable.

This sentence has brought me closer to the community I really serve. That's the radical view, the poor community. It's shown me what solidarity means. It's shown me what friendship means. It's shown me what love means. It's shown me what being a real human means, not standing by people when they're knocked down, not further knocking them down, not going after poor people if they want to provide for their families and not do it the way that the white society thinks is appropriate. You're disgusting.

Works like this one wouldn't be possible without the tireless work of translators and archivists like Mitchell Abidor, Matthew Lyons, Paul Sharkey, Nicholas Walter, Shawn Wilbur, George Woodcock, Hippolyte Havel, Sébastien Faure, Daniel Burton-Rose, theanarchistlibrary.org, Contagion Books, and the Labadie Collection.

# How Nonviolence Protects the State
# Peter Gelderloos

Since the civil rights era, the doctrine
of nonviolence has enjoyed near-
universal acceptance by the US Left.
Today protest is often shaped by
cooperation with state authorities—
even organizers of rallies against
police brutality apply for police
permits, and anti-imperialists
usually stop short of supporting
self-defense and armed resistance.
How Nonviolence Protects the
State challenges the belief that

nonviolence is the only way to fight for a better world. In a call
bound to stir controversy and lively debate, Peter Gelderloos
invites activists to consider diverse tactics, passionately arguing
that exclusive nonviolence often acts to reinforce the same
structures of oppression that activists seek to overthrow.

Peter Gelderloos is the author *The Failure of Nonviolence,
Worshiping Power: An Anarchist View of Early State
Formation, Diagnostic of the Future—Between the Crisis
of Democracy and the Crisis of Capitalism: A Forecast* and
*Anarchy Works: Examples of Anarchist Ideas in Practice.*

ISBN: 978-1948501019
Distributed by AK Press
198 pages; $12.00
detritusbooks.com

# Time & Time Again
## John Zerzan

These three essays were written about a dozen years apart, from the mid-'80s to 2017. I've been intrigued by the subject and so have returned to try again.

I think that it is with time—that is, our consciousness of this so-elusive object—that we first enter into a symbolic field or dimension. Our lives thus begin an estrangement that grows and grows. Time and alienation are two words that are the measure of each other. Time becomes a thing, standing pitilessly over us.

Taken together maybe these pieces are strands toward solving the puzzle of time. In my view the topic is best understood historically (and pre-historically) so as to ground and be able to chart its course.

Once we lived without time. Now it's all too real. But it was never a natural or inevitable development. A harbinger of symbolic culture...and look what that's brought us.

John Zerzan is the author of *A People's History of Civilization,* as well as a frequent contributor to *Fifth Estate* magazine and *Black and Green Review.*

ISBN: 978-1948501002
Distributed by AK Press
105 pages; $12.00
detritusbooks.com

# Contra el Leviatan y contra su historia
## Fredy Perlman

Con una mirada lúcida y subver-
siva, Fredy Perlman analiza el con-
junto de civilización, patriarcado y
Estado—la dominación en su total-
idad—desde sus orígenes hasta el
presente. Además, critica la forma en
que esta historia se nos ha enseñado,
destapando el poder del mito en una
sociedad racional y regalándonos
otra narrativa, desde abajo, que nos
habla de resistencia y libertad.

With a lucid and subversive view,
Fredy Perlman analyzes the whole of
civilization, patriarchy and State—domination in its entirety—
from its origins to the present. Also, he criticizes the way in
which this history has been taught to us, uncovering the power
of myth in a rational society and giving us another narrative,
from below, that speaks of resistance and freedom.

Published in English as *Against His-story, Against Leviathan!*
Fredy Perlman was co-founder of Black and Red Books, and
author of the books *Letters of Insurgents*, *The Continuing
Appeal of Nationalism*, *Worker-Student Action Committees:
France May '68*, as well as numerous essays, pamphlets and
contributions to *Fifth Estate* magazine.

ISBN: 978-1948501033
Distributed by AK Press
330 pages; $16.00
detritusbooks.com